I Hate the Lake District

Part of the Goldsmiths Press Unidentified Fictional Objects Series

I Hate the Lake District

Charlie Gere

Goldsmiths
Press

© 2019 Goldsmiths Press
Published in 2019 by Goldsmiths Press
Goldsmiths, University of London, New Cross
London SE14 6NW

Printed and bound by TJ International
Distribution by the MIT Press
Cambridge, Massachusetts, and London, England

A CIP record for this book is available from the British Library

ISBN 978-1-912685-11-0 (pbk)
ISBN 978-1-912685-12-7 (ebk)

www.gold.ac.uk/goldsmiths-press

Contents

Acknowledgements

Many thanks to Charlotte Fairbairn and Bronwen Riley for escapades in Cumbria and for pointing me in the direction of places to see, to Adam Sutherland, Alistair Hudson and all those involved with Grizedale Arts for shaping my understanding of the Lake District, to Jenn Ashworth, Fiona Candlin and Peter Davidson for taking the time to read draft material, and for their generous encouragement, to the anonymous readers for Goldsmiths Press for their positive reactions, to colleagues at Lancaster University and elsewhere for listening patiently to early versions of this book, and, above all, to my wife Lucinda for her superhuman tolerance.

'The Snow Party' from *New Collected Poems* (2011) by Derek Mahon appears by kind permission of the author and the Gallery Press, Loughcrew, Oldcastle, County Meath, Ireland. Poems from *Imaginary Postcards (Clints Grikes Grips Glints)* by Jonathan Williams appear by kind permission of the Literary Estate of Jonathan Williams. Excerpts from 'Briggflatts' by Basil Bunting from *Complete Poems* (2000), edited by Richard Caddell, appear by kind permission of Bloodaxe Books, 2000. The excerpt from 'St. Roach' in *The Collected Poems of Muriel Rukeyser*, Copyright © 2005 by Muriel Rukeyser, is reprinted by permission of ICM Partners. 'To the Stone-Cutters', 1924 and renewed 1952 by Robinson Jeffers from *The Selected Poetry of Robinson Jeffers* by Robinson Jeffers, used by permission of Random House, an imprint and division of Penguin Random House LLC. All rights reserved.

Acknowledgements

Introduction

The somewhat juvenile title of this book comes from the story about Malcolm McLaren's first encounter with John Lydon, later known as Johnny Rotten, who was wearing a Pink Floyd T-shirt with the words 'I Hate' written in biro at the top. It turns out that Lydon was always a fan of Pink Floyd's music, but hated the pomposity of the prog rock music culture the band epitomised. In the same way, I love the North West of England, but hate the 'Lake District', and the way it's fetishised and sacralised as some kind of 'unspoilt' paradise, a consolatory Eden to which those battered by contemporary life can retreat. I also love it, guiltily, for the very reasons that I hate it. I am overwhelmed, for example, by the experience of the mountains of the North Lakes in the autumn light, and uneasy that the pleasure I feel is a false appeal to 'nature' as redemptive. *I Hate the Lake District* is an attempt to deal with this unease and to present a different view of the Lake District and the North West of England to that found in most accounts. It is also an engagement with the problematic idea of 'nature' that seems to obsess certain contemporary writers, and their readers. The natural world, whatever that might be, is fetishised as a kind of redemptive alternative to the human world. Yet, of course, nature, as a concept, can exist only in a binary relation with that world. Outside of that relation it can have no meaning at all.

The origins of the book go back some years to a time when I found myself alone for several months. My wife was looking after family down south. After an initial period of adjustment and a certain amount of resentment, I grew to enjoy the freedom her absence gave me. What I particularly liked was the opportunity to do something that can really only be done alone; to go for long drives with no particular aim or to look at some sight that I had read about and that intrigued me. The area where these peregrinations took place was then mostly in Cumbria, and to a lesser extent in Lancashire and North Yorkshire.

There are precedents for this kind of writing, going back to Jean-Jacques Rousseau's *Reveries of the Solitary Walker*, and, more recently, the work of Yves Bonnefoy, W. G. Sebald, Iain Sinclair and Annie Dillard, among others. However, Rousseau, Sebald and Sinclair are walkers, and their writings are structured by the act of walking. Though I enjoy walking greatly, whether in the Lakes or elsewhere, the main form of mobility in this book is driving. In fact this book emerges out of the cinematic experience of driving through the Lakes and the North West of England, with the car windscreen acting as a kind of cinema screen, and the radio, tuned to BBC 6 Music, offering the soundtrack. Perhaps each chapter can be thought of as a kind of miniature road movie (even though the road movie is a not a genre that suits England much. The country is too small and too populated).

It was always with the intention of writing about them that I undertook these journeys. I wanted to write in the same way I wanted to travel, without plans, open to what may arrive, free to pursue connections however tenuous, and above all to enjoy the process of writing without the necessity of undertaking it for some prior purpose. To write like this is also to be free of the disciplinary demands of academia, which I had begun to find increasingly frustrating. Being, in every sense, undisciplined, I found that the increasing instrumentalisation of research was beginning to feel like a cage. Like Melville's *Bartleby the Scrivener*, I wished to say 'I would prefer not to' to such demands. I wanted to recover the stupidity of study. The Italian philosopher Giorgio Agamben makes the connection directly by claiming the etymology of the word *studium* goes back to a st- or sp- root, indicating 'a crash, the shock of an impact' and thus that studying and stupefying are akin. '[T]hose who study are in the situation of people who have received a shock and are stupefied by what has struck them, unable to grasp it and at the same time powerless to leave hold.'

Thus the 'scholar is always "stupid".' Agamben describes study as '*per se* interminable' and writes of those 'who are acquainted with long hours spent roaming among books, when every fragment, every codex, every initial encountered seems to open a new path, immediately left aside at the next encounter.'[1]

We had moved to the North West of England more than a decade before the journeys described, for me to take up a Readership at Lancaster University. That I should end up in such a place was, to say the least, surprising. I was born and brought up in a part of West London known as the World's End. Though the name derived from a coaching inn that had been in the area since the seventeenth century, it seemed suitably apocalyptic for the period of my childhood, that of 1960s and the 1970s and the Cold War. Back in the 1970s, London was a strange place, much emptier, and far more run down than it is now, in its current incarnation as the capital city of neo-liberalism and tax evasion. Accordingly, like many of my contemporaries, I was drawn to a certain cultural ethos and aesthetic, involving Punk Rock and New Wave music (especially New York New Wave), as well as that of David Bowie (of course), the films of Andrei Tarkovsky and David Lynch, the writing of J. G. Ballard, Don Delillo, Philip K. Dick and, later on, David Foster Wallace. Taken as a whole, these different sources offered a kind of bleak vision of a kind of post-apocalyptic culture. It was also a thoroughly urban vision, with little or no connection to ideas about 'nature' and the rural.

Being a city dweller was indeed part of my conception of myself, and I fully expected to spend my entire life in a city, most probably London. It was therefore as much of a surprise to me as to my friends when we moved to the deep north of England. What was even more surprising was that what I found there was far closer to the kind of urban ethos described above than I could ever have imagined. As Peter Davidson's wonderful book *The Idea of North* demonstrates, northern locations have often been thought of as strange and deathly places, realms of the dead and of mystery, and this remains true of the North West of England, for all its popularity as a holiday destination.[2] Cumbria was the limit of the Roman occupation, and also the furthest reach of empire, the greatest distance from Rome. Corbridge proudly boasts of having been the northernmost town of the Roman Empire. Bronwyn Riley's recent book *A Journey to Britannia* shows that getting to the far North West was not only a difficult and arduous business, but also a shift from the sunlit south to the mysterious, cloudy, rainy world of northern Europe.[3] The romantic landscapes of the Lake District or the Yorkshire Dales that have made the North West so attractive to visitors also meant that it was and remains difficult land from which to produce a living. Behind the tourist façade and tourist-friendly beauty that owes so much to William Wordsworth, the land remains hard, harsh and poor.

It is to Wordsworth that we owe the idea of the Lake District as paradise regained – as in the beginning of his long, unfinished poem, *The Recluse*, his response to Milton's *Paradise Lost*.

ONCE to the verge of yon steep barrier came
A roving school-boy; what the adventurer's age
now escaped his memory—but the hour
One of a golden summer holiday,
He well remembers, though the year be gone—
Alone and devious from afar he came;
And, with a sudden influx overpowered
At sight of this seclusion, he forgot
His haste, for hasty had his footsteps been
As boyish his pursuits; and sighing said,
'What happy fortune were it here to live!
And, if a thought of dying, if a thought
Of mortal separation, could intrude
With paradise before him, here to die!'[4]

Wordsworth was an incomparably great poet, and did the Lake District a great service in many ways by pointing out its extraordinary beauty. But, at the same time, in encouraging the general appreciation of that beauty, something has been lost. Even while Wordsworth was still alive, the area was already becoming 'Wordsworthshire', accessible by train and visited by a cultivated middle class in order to experience the sublimity and beauty of nature. In this way, the original Romantic vision of the Lakes became something far more sentimental, a kind of fetishisation of the natural scenery as an idyll and an escape from the urban and industrial.

Wordsworth can thus be seen to have initiated a long and continuing tradition of nature writing which treats the environment as a kind of balm or salve for our sick souls. This seems, if anything, to be more popular than ever, particularly in the new nature writing you see on tables in bookshops, with all those books by Robert McFarlane, Richard Mabey, Richard Deakin, Helen McDonald and others, which offer to a largely urban audience intelligent, beautifully written and sometimes somewhat reactionary visions of 'nature'.

Lying in the bath recently I noticed a hitherto unseen bath soak bottle next my prosaic *Head and Shoulders*, with the name *Faith in Nature*. This seemed to me to be as good a phrase as any for this kind of nature writing, in which a covert spirituality is implicit in the most material descriptions of the environment. 'Nature' becomes a source of religious feeling and even faith, in which we can soak, in an age when other such sources are no longer plausible. Even more apposite was the implication that such as faith could be reduced to a shampoo brand. (I also noticed another bottle, half concealed behind a shelf, with what I thought was a strangely appropriate name, *Paradox*, until I realised it was only *Radox*).

Perhaps the most famous poem about the Lake District is Wordsworth's 'I Wandered Lonely as a Cloud', also known as 'Daffodils'.

I wandered lonely as a cloud
That floats on high o'er vales and hill,

When all at once I saw a crowd,
A host, of golden daffodils;
Beside the lake, beneath the trees,
Fluttering and dancing in the breeze.[5]

This seems to be the epitome of the singularity and solitude of witnessing, and thus of what John Keats called Wordsworth's 'egoistical sublime'. For Australian poet John Kinsella, nature writing 'as a concept is too tied up with validating the relationship with the (Western!) notion of self, of egotistical sublime, of the gain the self has over the 'nature' s/he is relating to'.[6] To which one might add, it's almost always 'he'. As is well known, Wordsworth was not alone when he saw the sight that inspired the poem. He was, rather, walking with his sister, and he drew heavily on her account of the daffodils in her diary when writing 'Daffodils'. Dorothy's contribution to the poem, and indeed her very presence, is effaced in Wordsworth's desire to present the 'bliss of solitude' in his vision of the Lakes.

That kind of nature writing has a lot do with the legacy of Immanuel Kant, who claimed that we can only have access to objects as they appear to us, as '*phenomena*', not as they are in themselves, '*noumena*'. Kant described this as his 'Copernican revolution', comparable to Copernicus' rejection of the idea of the earth being the centre of the universe (except that it does the opposite and makes the human the source and centre of all knowledge). For Kant it is impossible to say anything about anything other than as it appears to us. Thus, in a sense, objects don't exist, other than in relation to the knowing human subject.

Nigel Clark connects Kant's thinking to his thrill and terror at the sheer contingency of terrestrial and celestial processes. For Kant, science revealed that the earth, like other planets, went through revolutions and paroxysms that had, in the case of the earth, obliterated earlier forms of life. Clark suggests that Kant recognised that 'the temporal and spatial dominion of our species was disturbingly inconsequential when viewed in the context of the earth's eventful history or the vastness of interplanetary space'. The very being that could 'process the phenomenal productions of physical reality, was at the same time one which was at risk of being overwhelmed by the exertions of the earth and cosmos' and was thus vulnerable to being swept away – which would leave the universe utterly devoid of any way of making sense of itself'.[7]

Kant's response was to 'to steer clear of what the turbulent forces of the universe could do on their own account, and fix our attention on our own interface with the world around us'.[8] Such thought 'has kept its focus firmly on the various achievements and potentialities of human agency, both in terms of our capacity to engage with each other and to articulate with the physical world around us'. Though it is likely that Wordsworth never read Kant, his thinking echoes that of the philosopher, as in this passage from the very end of the 1850 version of *The Prelude*, proclaiming the ultimate superiority of mind over nature.

Prophets of Nature, we to them will speak
A lasting inspiration, sanctified
By reason, blest by faith: what we have loved,
Others will love, and we will teach them how;
Instruct them how the mind of man becomes
A thousand times more beautiful than the earth
On which he dwells, above this frame of things
(Which, 'mid all revolution in the hopes
And fears of men, doth still remain unchanged)
In beauty exalted, as it is itself
Of quality and fabric more divine.[9]

Even when the narrator of the 1805 version of *The Prelude* encounters what we might call, in Kantian terminology, the Sublime, in the form of the 'huge Cliff', it becomes a means of asserting this superiority.

That spectacle, for many days, my brain
Work'd with a dim and undetermin'd sense
Of unknown modes of being; in my thoughts
There was a darkness, call it solitude,
Or blank desertion, no familiar shapes
Of hourly objects, images of trees,
Of sea or sky, no colours of green fields;[10]

But, despite this encounter with the unknown, Wordsworth is able to transform this negative moment, and others like it, by the 'higher power of imagination', discovering 'an immortal truth of being, as being in desire and hope', much as Kant can transform the experience of the sublime into something that affirms human freedom.

In some of his more recent work Robert McFarlane, often thought of as the poster boy of the New Nature Writing, shows increasing interest in a less anthropocentric approach to the environment, one that acknowledges the problem of its fundamental opacity. For example, writing about Nan Shepherd's forgotten masterpiece about the Cairngorms, *The Living Mountain*, MacFarlane confesses that she had 'remade' his vision of the mountains. One reason, perhaps, was that Shepherd did not treat the summit as the point of being on a mountain, something to be conquered, but rather that the mountain should be encountered on its own inhuman terms. McFarlane appreciates both the exhilaration and terror Shepherd feels at the mountain's 'mindlessness', and the degree to which the 'total mountain' could never be fully known. But, 'if approached without expectation' it was capable of offering 'remarkable glimpses into its being'.[11]

McFarlane seems to be straining towards another kind of representation of nature beyond that found in most nature writing, one that attempts to find the means to deal with 'nature' beyond our phenomenal apprehensions. Such an attempt is fraught with problems, and may prove impossible in the end. However, maybe in the context of our current environmental degradation we need to find some way of doing so. Eugene Thacker suggests that the 'world is increasingly unthinkable', in light of all the forms of ecological depredation, pollution and strange weather with which we are now faced, as well as the threat of actual extinction. For Thacker, this means our very capacity to understand the world is increasingly limited.[12]

He points out that this is not a new dilemma and that philosophy has 'repeatedly returned' to the problem of the nonhuman world. Thacker offers 'a new terminology' for this problem, distinguishing between the 'world-for-us', which is the world that we, as humans, live in, interpret, and find meaning and either relate to, or feel alienated from. This world often 'bites back' and resists our attempts to mould to our desires. The world that we can glimpse in this biting back is what Thacker calls 'the world-in-itself', which is the world in 'some inaccessible, already-given state, which we then turn into the world-for-us'.[13] The world-in-itself constitutes the limits of our thought, always going beyond what we can understand. Beyond the world-in-itself, according to Thacker, there is the 'world-without-us', which, unlike the world-in-itself, cannot co-exist with the 'human world-for-us'. It is the world in which we have been subtracted, and even to suggest that this world is antagonistic to us, is to still try to put things in human terms.[14]

In one of my favourite films, *Solaris*, Andrei Tarkovsky gives us a vision of the world-without-us. In *Archaeologies of the Future*, his book on science fiction and utopia, Fredric Jameson singles out the Stanislaw Lem novel on which Tarkovsky's film is based, as evidence of what he calls the 'unknowability thesis'.[15] In the novel and the film, Solaris is a remote planet covered with what appears to be an ocean. Almost all human scientific endeavour has now become devoted to trying to understand the planet, giving rise to the science of 'Solaristics', which, for some at least, has become a substitute for religion. However, despite these efforts, the planet resists any attempt to be understood. The ocean temporarily takes the form of immense spatial phenomena, some of which, resembling mountains, islands and fantastic architecture, can be explored. But these seem to be without meaning. Finally, out of frustration at the ocean's opacity, the humans surveying from the space station above bombard it with X-rays. The planet's response is to have 'visitors' appear on the space stations, perfect simulacra of figures from the occupants' often guilty past. Jameson suggests that even to ask the question of whether the ocean is punishing or torturing the occupants by presenting them with these revenants is to be stuck in a human frame of reference. Thus, Lem's message is 'that in imagining ourselves to be attempting contact with the radically Other, we are in reality merely looking in a mirror and "searching for an ideal image of our world"'. The bombardment of the ocean 'is not merely self-defeating but even suicidal, for in order to strip away the anthropomorphism, we must somehow do away with ourselves'.[16]

Solaris brilliantly skewers one of humankind's more comic anxieties: that we are somehow 'alone' in the universe because we have not yet encountered or been contacted by some entity that resembles us to some degree. This curious narcissism that can only imagine companionship with that which mirrors our own vain conception of consciousness is exemplified in bad science fiction, *Star Wars*, *Star Trek*, etc., in which, at worse, aliens are just humans with a bit of prosthetic make up and, at best, animatronic or CGI-generated creatures. Given the contingency of evolution, the chances of another species like us developing or even life as we understand it emerging elsewhere are practically nil. *Solaris* confronts us with the prospect that any encounter with another 'consciousness' is likely to be radically other. We do not even need to leave the planet to have such encounters. As the novelist Richard Powers remarked in a recent interview in *The Guardian*, the idea that the environment that surrounds us is just property is deeply alienating. As he puts it:

Every form of mental despair and terror and incapacity in modern life seems to be related in some way to this complete alienation from everything else alive. We're deeply, existentially lonely. Until it's exciting and fun and ecstatic to think that everything else has agency and is reciprocally connected we're going to be terrified and afraid of death, and it's mastery or nothing.[17]

Powers limits his sense of connectivity to living things, in particular trees. In conversation with Lucien Price, Alfred North Whitehead talked of the way that even a rock is extraordinarily lively, a 'raging mass of activity', however static it might appear.[18] This applies to anything and everything: trees, humans, rocks, metal, plastic, air, etc.

Barbara Ehrenreich, in her eminently sane recent publication *Natural Causes: Life, Death and the Illusion of Control*, finds consolation in the thought that everything that exists is the result of quantum fluctuations, most of which are transient but some of which 'occur simultaneously and glom together to form a building block of matter, perhaps leading, in a few billion years, to a new universe'. She suggests that this leads to an insight known to our animist ancestors, but lost sight of 'in the last few hundred years of rigid monotheism, science, and Enlightenment'.

And that is the insight that the natural world is not dead, but swarming with activity, sometimes even agency and intentionality. Even the place where you might expect to find quiet and solidity, the very heart of matter – the interior of a proton or a neutron – turns out to be animated with the ghostly flickerings of quantum fluctuations. I would not say the universe is 'alive,' since that might invite misleading biological analogies. But it is restless, quivering, juddering, from its vast vacant patches to its tiniest crevices.[19]

However, what prevents us from embracing this vision of a vibrant universe and makes death such an 'intolerant prospect' is the monstrous self that 'occludes our vision' and 'separates us from other beings'. We need to do what most fail to, which is to get beyond the self, the 'I'.

The Buddhist writer John McClellan, in an article for the Buddhist journal *Triangle* entitled 'Nondual Ecology', attacks those deep ecologists who are happy to recognise the 'inherent buddha nature of rocks and clouds', but take technology to be inherently evil. For such ecologists, 'recognizing this prized quality of aliveness in technology, in human/machine interaction, and in abstract symbolic systems is something else again. Buddha-nature in nuclear bombs? In computer systems, in our urban networks, in the workings of pure mathematics? No one in the environmental world seems willing to go that far; only cyberpunks and techno-futurists have such thoughts, and they are generally dismissed as frivolous by us serious, "nature"-loving Deep Ecologists. We Buddhists, and Muirists, and Thoreauists'.[20]

Thus, 'they would like to exclude certain things, exploitive technology, warfare, social injustice, famine, urban landscape, television, the extinction of non competitive species, the collapse of planetary life support systems for higher species...' He finds a better view in the work of Whitman, Blake and Rumi, and those Zen and Tibetan teachers, for all of whom 'all of Life is honored impartially, devils and angels together, on their own scary terms'.[21] This is what he calls a Nondual Ecology, in which 'all forms of life are honored equally' including 'anything that displays neg-entropic activity, i.e. the self-organizing, information encoding, entropy defying activity of dissipative structures, as described by Ilya Prigogine and others in the field of Complexity'. From his Buddhist perspective, everything is sentient.

Sentient Being itself looms up, vast, inconceivable, glowing and humming, in all ages and all spaces—indestructible, beyond confusing particulars. This vast Presence of aliveness, of sentient Is-ness, filling the time-space cosmos from beginning to end, dwarfs all bodhisattvas, all saints, revolutionaries, and liberal reformers—it silences the poets, and overflows even the hearts of mothers. It is inexhaustible, self-sufficient, needing nothing, wanting nothing. Suffering is as natural and organic a process to it as breathing. The tides of life and death are its diastolic rhythm.[22]

There is nothing to be saved, nothing to be preserved. For McClellan, we must not cling onto notions of how things should be. 'Sound ecology must be based on respect for evolution's creative/destructive working process, not on a childish clinging to pretty toys it may have made. Then we can live in this world, help it out, and *lean into* its mysterious unfolding.'[23] For McLennan, 'everything moves', from 'mindless hydrogen clouds swirling purposelessly in interstellar spacetime, to clouds of thoughts swirling around in the brain' and thus demonstrates 'inherent aliveness'. Everything is also 'beautiful to behold, including the ugly ones, all are precious, including the worthless ones, all are friends & relatives, even the dangerous ones, even when they kill you!'[24]

What McClellan describes is very close to the ethical nihilism that philosophers such as Brian Snyder understand to be a necessary concomitant of Darwinian materialism. In Singer's words, 'in a materialistic worldview, there is no basis for value of either human or non-human life'. Any attempt to prescribe such value is either metaphysical or religious, or 'a function of the philosopher's desire to influence the world, that is, the will to power'.[25] (This is where Richard Dawkins makes his most egregious error, in believing, as a Darwinist, he can make value judgements about phenomena such as religion and science.) It is also similar to the 'vehement antinaturalism' proclaimed in the *Xenofeminist Manifesto*. Xenofeminism offers a new form of feminism. 'Anyone who's been deemed "unnatural" in the face of reigning biological norms, anyone who's experienced injustices wrought in the name of natural order, will realize that the glorification of "nature" has nothing to offer us—the queer and trans among us, the differently-abled, as well as those who have suffered discrimination due to pregnancy or duties connected to child-rearing. XF is vehemently anti-naturalist. Essentialist naturalism reeks of theology—the sooner it is exorcised, the better.[26] As Slavoj Žižek puts it, 'if there is one good thing about capitalism, it is that, precisely, mother earth now no longer exists.'[27]

The question is how to engage with this liveliness that is so other to the human. Such an engagement is, necessarily, hard. However, this is not to say that people have not tried. Long before science fiction presented us with visions of unknowability, the desert offered a (non)space for possible confrontation with God or nothingness, '*Deus sive Nihil*.'[28] The desert, as profoundly inimical to human life, makes it possible to confront the fragility and absolute contingency of our existence, our own fundamental decentredness and nothingness, which in turn offers the possibility of experiencing something beyond human access. At the same time of course, such a vision of the desert remains thoroughly anthropocentric, disavowing its complexity in lieu of its inhospitality towards us. Nevertheless, the desert can offer an idea of what seeing beyond the limits of human consciousness might be like. In *Desert Solitaire*, his description of his time as a ranger in the Utah desert, Edward Abbey writes that being alone for a long time 'means risking everything human.'[29] He also proclaims his desire to confront what he describes as 'the bare bones of existence', to look at a juniper tree, a piece of quartz, a vulture, a spider, and 'see it as it is in itself', without any humanly ascribed qualities, in an entirely anti-Kantian manner.[30]

Of course, even to give a name to something and to imagine that that named thing can be seen without 'humanly ascribed qualities' is contradictory. Its existence as a thing in the first place is a human construct. If one was able to glimpse behind the phenomenal veil, it is likely that what was perceived would be impossible to put into words. This is what Adam Roberts engages with in his wittily entitled novel *The Thing Itself*, which combines a reference to Stephen King's horror novel *The Thing* with Kant's notion of the *noumenon*, the thing itself. In the novel, the avowedly atheist Roberts stages a dialogue between his protagonist, a scientist and also an atheist, and an advanced artificial intelligence, in which Kant is used as an argument for believing in God. The scientist, whose name is Charles, has glimpsed what he believes to be, in Kantian terms, the Thing Itself, or in other words the plenitude of noumenal reality. This takes place in an Arctic research station where Charles is stuck with Roy, an eccentric colleague obsessed with Kant and with using computer technology to access the Real. However, it is Charles, having been locked out of the station by Roy, who actually does. He describes what he encounters as:

Data experience of a radically new kind. Raw tissues of flesh, darkness visible, a kind of fog (no: fog is the wrong word). A pillar of fire by night, except that 'it' did not burn, or gleam, or shine. 'It' is the wrong word for it. 'It' felt, or looked, like a great tumbling of scree down an endless slope. Or rubble gathering at the bottom and falling up the mountain. Forwards, backwards'.[31]

Here, Roberts tries to imagine the literally unimaginable (or at least tries to imagine someone imagine the unimaginable). This is similar to what Simone Weil calls 'decreation'. Weil sees herself as interposing her subjectivity, herself, between God and his Creation, like 'an unwelcome third who is between two betrothed lovers and ought to go away so they can really be together'. Weil declares, 'If only I could see a landscape as it is when I am not there. But when I am in any place I disturb the silence of heaven by the beating of my heart'.[32]

Cumbria, even when it is not being flooded, is prone to long, dark, wet winters. However, the return we get for this, and for end of winter arriving later than in much of the rest of England, is that spring is a delirious awakening that never fails to catch me out. It offers a shattering experience of beauty. I use the word shattering here carefully, to suggest that such an experience shatters the idea that the world is any way really for us, or that we can truly understand and master it, or that we are somehow at its centre.

Such beauty is profoundly indifferent to us. Something of this can sometimes be found in great art. It reminds me of what Weil says in her essay 'The Love of God and Affliction'. For Weil, true love of beauty is only possible through a renunciation of each person's imaginary position at the centre of the universe, an emptying out of our false divinity. Weil asks us to submit to the blind necessity of the universe, much as matter does, which is 'entirely passive and in consequence entirely obedient to God's will'.[33] She asks, '[W]hat is more beautiful than the action of gravity on the fugitive folds of the sea waves, or on the almost eternal folds of the mountains?'. She continues that:

The sea is not less beautiful in our eyes because we know that sometimes ships are wrecked by it. On the contrary this adds to its beauty. If it altered the movement of its waves to spare a boat, it would be a creature gifted with discernment and choice and not this fluid, perfectly obedient to every external pressure. It is this perfect obedience that constitutes the sea's beauty.[34]

The experience of the environment's utter indifference is a particularly edifying experience in the context of a culture that is always concerned with seducing us to consume, using our senses as a means of marketing. Such experience is, in the end, unrepresentable; no painting, no photograph, no verbal description can adequately convey what it is like. Indeed, all such descriptions fail because they presuppose a subject looking out onto what he or she sees, as something separate, rather than the actuality, that we are also part of what we see, and our seeing is what makes it possible. It is this that forecloses the possibility of thinking of what we are experiencing as something separate to us called 'nature'. We, and all we do and make, are part of 'nature', which is therefore everything and thus nothing at all. This beauty is also shattering because it is terrifying, partly because it implies the extraordinary excess of energy needed to create all that exists.

A minute glimpse of this is possible in the profuse growth of flowers that suddenly proliferate, the riotous growth in meadows and alongside roads of weeds and grasses, the vibrating life of animals and so on.

This kind of desubjectification is explored by Hugo von Hofmannsthal, in his short work *The Lord Chandos Letter* in which he imagines his fictional peer explain to Francis Bacon (the seventeenth-century philosopher) that he is losing the ability to use language. However, this is a situation which is not without its pleasurable moments, but which are not nameable. These include:

A watering can, a harrow left in a field, a dog in the sun, a shabby church-yard, a cripple, a small farmhouse—any of these can become the vessel of my revelation. Any of these things and the thousand similar ones past which the eye ordinarily glides with natural indifference can at any moment—which I am completely unable to elicit—suddenly take on for me a sublime and moving aura which words seem too weak to describe.[35]

For the novelist Enrique Vila-Matas, the Letter 'represents a manifesto of the passing away of the word, the shipwreck of the ego, in the convulsed and indistinct flow of things which can no longer be named or tamed by language.'[36]

In his book *Remnants of Auschwitz: The Witness and the Archive*, Giorgio Agamben quotes from a letter from John Keats to Richard Woodhouse (whom Agamben curiously misnames as John Woodhouse). Though Agamben does not mention it, it is in this letter that Keats clearly distinguishes his own kind of poet-ical character from what he calls the 'wordsworthian or egotistical sublime'. Agamben singles out five paradoxical theses in Keats' 'wretched confession' about the continuous loss of self, the alien-ation and non-existence, which make up the poetic subject. The first is that the 'I' of poetic discourse is not an I, is not identical with itself – it has no self. The second is that the poet is the most unpoetical thing, as he is always other than himself. Thirdly, the statement 'I am a poet' is a contradiction in terms, given that the poet has no self. Fourthly, the poetic experience involves the experience of desubjectification. The fifth and final paradoxical thesis is that, despite the above, the poet will continue to write, because of 'the promise of an absolute and unfailing writing destined to destroy and renew itself every day'. Agamben suggests that it is as if the shame and desubjectification implicit in the act of speech contained a 'secret beauty that could only bring the poet incessantly to bear witness to his own alienation'.[37]

Agamben claims that in the Western literary tradition, the 'act of poetic creation and, indeed, every act of speech implies something like a desubjectification', or what the poets call the 'Muse'. Thus, the desubjectification of which the poet is aware is actually a condition of any form of speech at all, inasmuch as the statement 'I speak' is as contradictory as 'I am a poet'.[38]

For me, the exemplary fiction about witnessing the unrepresentable and the concomitant desubjectification of the subject is Jeff Vandermeer's *Southern Reach* trilogy, the first volume of which, *Annihilation*, was published in 2014.[39] The *Southern Reach* trilogy features a Zone, not unlike that found in Tarkovsky's *Stalker*. Some thirty years before the beginning of the first book, an area of the south-west coast of the United States has suffered some mysterious environmental breakdown, possibly caused by some alien force. Known as Area X, it has been closed off by the military and is now monitored by a secret agency known as the Southern Reach. Periodically, expeditions are sent into the area, all of which end in one form of disaster or another. The first book is largely concerned with what we – and those on the exhibition – are led to believe is the twelfth expedition (though there have, in fact, been many more), and in particular, the fate of the character known simply as the biologist. Names are abandoned in Area X. Vandermeer offers a brilliant vision of a deeply uncanny and unknowable landscape as witnessed by the biologist, in which the very laws of nature are overturned and what the group witnesses is beyond their capacity to understand or represent. The recent film of *Annihilation*, though it changed the plot somewhat, beautifully captured the sense of strangeness of Area X, as described in the book.

David Tompkins compares the *Southern Reach* trilogy not just to H. P. Lovecraft, J. G. Ballard and *Stalker* and *Solaris* but also to 'the American naturalist tradition running from Thoreau, Rachel Carson and Annie Dillard to, more recently, David Quammen and Elizabeth Kolbert.'[40] He points out how at certain points Thoreau and Dillard's writing becomes weird. Joshua Rothman picked up on this to dub Vandermeer as the 'weird Thoreau.'[41] Unlike Lovecraft's fear and anxiety about the horrors he invokes, for Tompkins Vandermeer 'embrace[s] all these things' and presents 'an ecologically minded Weird fiction' in which 'Area X is not a channel into the primordial ooze where tentacled, bloblike Old Ones lurk (*à la* Lovecraft)'. Area X is frightening, not because it is 'a reversion to Chaos and Old Night but... the start of a comprehensive reversal of the Anthropocene Age.'[42]

Tompkins suggests that Vandermeer 'imaginatively merges the naturalist and un-naturalist traditions', and that the biologist represents this merger, and comes to practice a kind of weird ecology, 'one fit for our moment, when we've begun to understand that what is happening in the world, to the world, is happening irreversibly'. He quotes the ecological literary critic Timothy Morton on what Morton calls the hyperobject, a phenomenon that is massively distributed in time and space relative to humans, the apprehension of which reveals to us our fundamental interobjectivity with every other thing in the world.[43] 'The reality is that hyperobjects were already here, and slowly but surely we understood what they were already saying. They contacted us.' For Tompkins, the books in the trilogy 'imaginatively figure this contact' in 'that they let the other side win' and 'offer a collapsitarianism in reverse.'[44] Thus, 'Area X represents not ecological collapse but rather human collapse – or, better said, human transmutation' by cleansing 'its territory of anthropogenic poisoning, then sets to work on people themselves'. Tompkins quotes 'one of more unhinged employees of the Southern Reach': 'Would that not be the final humbling of the human condition? That the trees and birds, the fox and the rabbit, the wolf and the deer... reach a point at which they do not even notice us, as we are transformed'.[45]

It is this weird ecology that Vandermeer's novels embody that I would like to see manifested in writing about areas such as the Lake District. Perhaps this can be seen in terms of putting the Lake District under erasure, by crossing it out as a name with a big X, which is also, of course, a homage to Vandermeer's area X. Or even, following Michel Foucault, an X through the human so 'that man would be erased, like a face drawn in sand at the edge of the sea'.[46] This would involve an acknowledgement of the violence and contingency, the hyper-chaos, of 'nature', its fundamental turbulence and unknowability. Above all, it would acknowledge how 'we' are no more than another aspect of this violence and contingency, another ephemeral phenomenon in an unimaginably long and complex process of evolution.

The environment that we are concerned with saving or sustaining is the one to which we have access, the one which sustains us. Outside of the anthropocentric bubble there is no reason to value some forms of existence over others, or even to presume on the value of life over non-life, whatever that distinction even means. As Nietzsche puts it, 'Let us beware of saying that death is opposed to life. The living is only a form of what is dead, and a very rare form'.[47] Beyond my own selfish, human concerns, what reason is there to value the existence of a particular species of bird, over that of a deadly virus or a desert of rock and sand? There is also a negative anthropocentrism in play in relation to our responses to global warming, in which a pristine, stable, benevolent environment, the 'planet', is ruined by the intervention of a disordered, fallen humanity, as if coming from somewhere outside. Nigel Clark's point is that the 'planet' is already a violently contingent and disruptive environment, and has been long before the advent of humanity. This is in no way to deny global warming, but rather to understand it as part of an always already violent 'nature'.

I believe that, at the heart of much of our concern with the environment, and our obsession with sustainability, is a fear of death. It is part of what Ernest Becker famously characterised as our 'denial of death'. Barbara Ehrenreich critiques this denial and suggests that we cease to fight death, and find ways to accept it instead. For me, this means accepting not just our own death but the end or death of everything with which we are surrounded, including our environment. This means, at its most radical, embracing the plastic in the ocean, the asbestos in the dumps, the radiation on our hills, as much as the fauna and flora of 'nature'.

The flooding in Cumbria in 2015 with Storm Desmond really brought home to me and to many others the violence of nature. All winter it had rained relentlessly, even before the flooding. It already felt as if there was nothing but rain, as if rain was the only atmospheric condition we had. Every day and all night the rain fell, and fell. The idea of a day or night without rain seemed unimaginable, or a kind of half memory. But early in December the rain took on a new violence. No longer simply falling, it now danced chaotically in the sky, passing horizontally and diagonally, as much as vertically. I had to drive to Coniston that day for a meeting. Perhaps I shouldn't have gone, shouldn't have taken the risk. Still, I did go. All along the A65 from Kirkby Lonsdale torrents flowed across the road from the higher to the lower fields. Cars waited in queues so that one car at a time from either direction could pass in the middle of the road, at the point where the water was the shallowest. Many cars were stalled in the middle of the flooded roads. On the A590 there were frequent points at which the police had to direct drivers around fallen branches or landslipped walls. The road from Greenodd to Coniston was nearly impassable, so deep were the impromptu rivers flowing over its width. It began to feel as if the world was liquefying, or as if the solidity of things was now being dispelled. Water seemed to be the real material of the world, and was busy reclaiming all that had been saved from its grasp.

When I got back home, the house was not itself flooded, though the garden was now mostly a fast-flowing stream. These were repeats of the great Cumbrian floods of 2009, then declared to be a once-in-a-lifetime event. This time the damage seemed even worse. The A591 was completely impassable beyond Grasmere. From newspaper images it looks as if a giant had taken great bites out of its side. Every house on the main street into Carlisle had been affected by the water, and later, almost every one would be boarded up, waiting to be repaired. Months after, those who had to leave their houses on the low-lying parts of Kendal, near the River Kent, were still unable to move back. For a considerable time, the floods were the main topic of conversation at any social gathering. Everybody has war stories about flooded houses or irreparably damaged cars.

All this is a reminder that the Lakes were once under water. The oldest part of the Lake District is the Skiddaw Group of rocks, in the north of the National Park, which were formed 'as black muds and sands settling on the seabed about 500 million years ago', since when they have been, in the words of the Lake District National Park website, 'raised up and crumpled and squeezed'. Three hundred and twenty million years ago, a tropical sea covered the whole Lake District, out of which the remains of unimaginably large numbers of minute sea animals formed the outcrops of limestone found all over the area.[48] They may be inundated again sometime in the future. Our conception of our environment needs a greater sense of the great stretches of time in which it exists beyond our human conception, and our own ephemerality.

When undertaking the journeys that I describe in this book I was haunted, or perhaps beguiled, by a fantasy of the North West of England somehow becoming deserted. I imagined this coming about through a number of science fiction scenarios; the whole area being made uninhabitable by an accident at Sellafield; an alien invasion as in *Stalker*; or even something entirely inexplicable, as in the *Southern Reach* trilogy. We know, through books such as Alan Weisman's *The World Without Us*, that without the continual presence of humans much if not all of the infrastructure of any area, 'natural' and otherwise, would soon succumb to entropic chaos.[49] In towns, pavements would crack under the pressure of temperature fluctuations and proliferating plant growth. Without maintenance, buildings would be undermined and collapse. The materials with which we surround ourselves would rapidly rot and disintegrate. In the rural areas, all the human-derived cultivation would be overwhelmed by other more robust vegetation. Wild animals would overwhelm any domestic species and flourish. Much of this can already be seen in zones such as Chernobyl, the Demilitarized Zone between the two Koreas and other areas that have been abandoned, for one reason or another, by humans.

If there were no human presence in the Lake District, the irony is that it would, over time, become the 'unspoilt natural wilderness' that we are supposed to believe it already is. The Lake District is of course as much a purely human artefact as any city. I doubt many of those who fetishise the supposed natural and unspoilt beauty of the area would like or appreciate it if it was genuinely 'rewilded'. Much of what we prize as natural is thoroughly mediated by human activity and presence. Part of the point here is that if the Lake District was truly deserted by humans, then there would be no presence, no witness for it to appear as wild, natural, unspoilt or otherwise.

In his brief account of his development as a writer, the Welsh poet John Barnie describes how he cured his unease at the 'speeded up chaos of modern change' and concomitant displacement. Part of his cure was reading about evolutionary biology. For Barnie, to 'descend imaginatively into what is sometimes called the deep time of geology' is to 'realise how temporary and provisional everything human is'.[50] Language, with which Barnie has been in love all his life, only emerged at the earliest two hundred thousand years ago, which is both 'an immense tract of time' and 'no time at all'.[51] As Barnie points out, for almost all of the 'three-and-a-half-thousand-million-years of life on Earth there has been no language, and no conscious mind capable of reflecting on it and celebrating it'.[52] He goes on to suggest that 'there will come a time perhaps sooner than we would wish, when this will be so again: extinction is the fate of all species and it will be that of our own'.[53] Nor is there any point looking to poetry or literature for any kind of immortality. However, Barnie does proclaim the necessity of poetry as something the human mind demands, even in adverse circumstances, a demand that 'we play with language again and again'. He continues that:

Nothing we build, nothing we say or think, will survive deep time. That's how it is. We are, as Robert Lowell wrote in the Epilogue to *Day by Day*, 'poor passing facts'. All the more reason to sing in all the languages we have. And afterwards, silence. Life on Earth shaping itself to the conformity that existed before us for three and a half billion years. The rustle of leaves; the susurrus of insect wings; the barking of something, somewhere across the sands.[54]

Sellafield

I decided to find a Japanese garden I had read about that still exists in the Eskdale Valley. The idea of such a garden in Cumbria seemed to me to be vastly incongruous, and, yet, in some way appropriate, though at the time of setting out I was not sure why. The drive to Eskdale and West Cumbria was long, past the Lyth Valley with its great cliff exiled from the sea that once covered the whole of the peninsula, and over Newby Bridge, through Ulverston and Broughton-in-Furness before turning onto the A595 to wind and snake my way up the west coast. The whole of that part of the country, the Furness Peninsula and the Cumbrian coast, is strangely compelling. It is on the edge in so many ways, in Cumbria but not part of the Lake District. As you drive through it, the Lake District is usually visible on your right, tantalising in its drama and sublimity. As always, while driving, I suffer from a kind of traveller's yearning – to turn off from the route I am taking and see what is at the end of another road or over a hill.

The drive took me round Duddon Sands, a little bite in the side of coast, just above Walney Island, and then around Black Combe. This is a comparatively low hill, but notable for its wide prospect, looking down over the coast and sea. Later I looked up what Wordsworth had to say about Black Combe in his *Guide to the Lakes*. He described it as 'the solitary Mountain Black Comb [sic], the summit of which, as that experienced surveyor, Colonel Mudge, declared, commands a more extensive view than any point in Britain. Ireland he saw more than once, but not when the sun was above the horizon.'[1] In 1811, in the context of the Napeolonic Wars and in the face of possible national defeat, the view from Black Combe is proclaimed by Wordsworth as a form of nation-building transcendence.

THIS Height a ministering Angel might select:
For from the summit of BLACK COMB (dread name
Derived from clouds and storms!) the amplest range
Of unobstructed prospect may be seen
That British ground commands:

He continues to describe what can be seen from the summit,
including

Gigantic mountains rough with crags; beneath,
Right at the imperial station's western base
Main ocean, breaking audibly, and stretched
Far into silent regions blue and pale;—

before concluding

Look homeward now!
In depth, in height, in circuit, how serene
The spectacle, how pure!—Of Nature's works,
In earth, and air, and earth-embracing sea,
A revelation infinite it seems.[2]

Driving beyond Black Combe, I turned east and followed
small roads to a small village named Eskdale Green, which sits
along a road on the side of a valley. Here, at the end of the village,
a notice points the way to the Japanese Garden through a passage
named Giggle Alley. To get to the garden I climbed up to a small
meadow in woodlands, which a notice informs the visitor were
much damaged in the storms of 2008, and then up stone steps to
a kind of glade in which, indeed, there is a Japanese garden, albeit
overgrown. There is bamboo in some profusion and maple trees
with their characteristic red leaves, though I could not see the
magnolia supposedly also present. There are the remains of pools,
empty as it has been dry, stones to cross streams, benches, little

bridges and in the middle a larger, characteristically Japanese, bridge with a pronounced arch. The day was one of clear blue light, and the glade seemed filled with that light. The unusual wea-ther (for Cumbria at least) enhanced the strangeness of finding the garden in this remote location.

The Japanese garden and the surrounding glades and wood-land areas were designed and built in 1914 by the famous garden designer Thomas Mawson for Lord Rea, a Liverpool coal and shipping magnate, who had already built Gate House, an Arts and Crafts mansion, nearby. In this period, Japanese gardens were fashionable and an aspect of a more general fascination with Japan, especially since it had opened up to the rest of the world in the middle of the last century. Visiting the garden offers a kind of dream of a kind of idealised Japan.

Japan had isolated itself from the rest of the world following the disastrous attempts by Catholic missionaries to convert the country to Christianity in the sixteenth and seventeenth cen-turies. After this isolation was decreed in 1638, only the Dutch were allowed to trade, from a single trading post. Foreigners who entered and Japanese who left the country and returned would both be subject to the death penalty. In *Moby-Dick*, reflecting on his experience as a whaler in the seas near Japan, Herman Melville described the Pacific as containing 'milky-ways of coral isles, and low-lying, endless, unknown archipelagoes, and impenetrable Japans'.[3] In his book on the Japanese tradition in English and American literature, Earl Miner suggests that, for Melville:

Japan and Moby Dick alike rise with great beauty from the blue depths of the Japanese seas, both with outward beauty but fundamentally unknown, unexplored, and inimical. Both challenge the heart of man only to destroy it.[4]

After the American naval Commander Matthew Perry forced the Japanese to open their country to the rest of the world in 1860, it became possible to engage properly with Japanese culture. The architect William Burges found the Japanese furniture he saw at the International Exhibition of 1862 to exemplify the ideals he sought in the artefacts of the Middle Ages. His colleague Josiah Conder, having worked in Burges' office, went to Japan to practise architecture, and also to study and write about Japanese painting, flower arranging and gardens. The book he wrote on the last topic, *Landscape Gardening in Japan*, published in 1871, was an important influence on gardeners in this country in adopting Japanese methods and aesthetics.

Much art and literature of the late nineteenth and early twentieth centuries was influenced by newly accessible Japanese writing, printmaking and architecture, from the writings of Lafcadio Hearn, to the Japanese influence on Aestheticism, *Japonisme*, the work of Whistler, Swinburne, and the Impressionists (who were greatly taken by Japanese prints), and onto the poetic languages made possible by the ideas of Ernest Fenellosa and most brilliantly developed by Ezra Pound and the Imagists. Japan, like other non-Western cultures, offered new forms of sensibility and thinking that were crucial to the critical project of artistic Modernism. The haiku, the short poem of three lines, of five, seven and five syllables, respectively, seemed in particular to enable a rethinking of poetics as something far more immediate. The most famous exponent of the haiku, and indeed the developer of its modern form, was the seventeenth-century poet Matsuo Basho.

When I got back home, I found my old Penguin Classics copy of Matsuo Basho's great work *The Narrow Road to the Deep North*. In the spring of 1689, Basho set out on a journey to the northern interior of Japan, composing poetry in the form then known as 'hokku', though later renamed in the late nineteenth century as 'haiku'. A couple of years later, he wrote an account of this journey which was published under the title *Oku no Hosomichi*, which could be translated as *The Narrow Road to the Interior*, but we generally know as *The Narrow Road to the Deep North*. This is how it starts.

Days and months are the travellers of eternity. So are the years that pass by. Those who steer a boat across the sea, or drive a horse over the earth till they succumb to the weight of years, spend every minute of their lives travelling. There are a great number of the ancients, too, who died on the road. I myself have been tempted for a long time by the cloud-moving wind – filled with a strong desire to wander.[5]

Describing Basho's journey to the far north of Japan, the text is also an account of his attempt to achieve enlightenment and to overcome the duality between subject and object. In this context, and in the Japanese imaginary, the far north is an austere place of danger and poverty, with farmers attempting to make a living from difficult conditions and bandits preying on travellers. Obviously, coming up the M6 to the North West of England in the early twenty-first century is not the same thing at all, but I always feel there is a sort of resonance, and that where we live is a kind of 'deep north', beyond the metropolitan centres of Liverpool and Manchester, and, on the other side of the country from the comparatively crowded and urbanised North East.

I remember going to an exhibition a year or so ago at the Wordsworth Trust in Grasmere devoted to Basho and Wordsworth as 'walking poets'. Though, for me, it is hard to think of poetry less alike than Wordsworth's epic works such as *The Prelude* and Basho's haiku, I suppose both can be seen to share a responsiveness to nature and the environment, and a yearning for untamed scenery such as both found in the northern parts of their respective countries. However, it is possible to suggest a crucial difference between them, emerging from their different religious backgrounds. Wordsworth inherits a notion of plenitude from his implicit pantheism, whereas Basho is more concerned with a Buddhist notion of emptiness, and of dependent arising and cessation.

In his strange book about Japan, *The Empire of Signs*, Roland Barthes points out that cities based on grids make us uncomfortable, in that they lack a centre to go to and return from. He suggests that this is well understood in the West, for historical, economic, religious and military reasons, and its cities are, in general, concentric. This is also a model of Western metaphysics, 'for which every center is the site of truth, the center of our cities are always full', and is where 'the values of civilization are gathered and condensed' in the form of churches, offices, banks, stores and promenades.[6] To go to the city centre is 'to encounter the social "truth," to participate in the proud plenitude of "reality". By contrast, Tokyo possesses a centre which is empty, being occupied by the imperial palace, which hides the 'sacred "nothing" '.[7]

Barthes imagines Japan as a kind of 'fictive nation', through which he can overcome the tyranny of meaning and signification that characterises the West.[8] Along with Japanese food, theatre and gestures such as bowing, the haiku is, for Barthes, an exemplary means of defeating the drive to meaning, and to halt language's continuous babble, to break its vicious infinity.[9] With the haiku, 'meaning is only a flash, a slash of light', which 'illumines, reveals nothing: it is the flash of the photograph one takes very carefully (in the Japanese manner) but having neglected to load the film'.[10]

The sense of ephemerality is not only an aspect of Basho's Buddhism, but also a reflection of a greater sense of the danger and contingency of nature. We all know of course that Japan was and indeed remains greatly vulnerable to earthquakes. In Japanese mythology, earthquakes are caused by the *Namazu* or *Onamazu*, a giant catfish that lives under the mud, and is guarded by the god Kashima, who restrains him with a stone. When the stone is removed the *Namazu* thrashes about, causing earthquakes. Following an earthquake in Edo (Tokyo) in 1855, the catfish started to be worshipped as a god of world rectification (*yonaishi daimyojin*).

One of the places that Basho passed through during his journey to the deep north was Fukushima Prefecture. Fukushima is of course the location of the catastrophic nuclear accident that occurred in 2011, the effects of which are still being endured. It was caused by the Great East Japan Earthquake, of magnitude 9.0, and with an epicentre 130 kilometres off-shore from the city of Sendai, in the Miyagi Prefecture on the eastern coast of the Japanese mainland, which occurred at 2.46 pm on 11 March of that year. The rare double quake lasted three minutes, and caused a tsunami, involving an area of seafloor 650 kilometres in length running north to south, moving between ten and twenty metres horizontally. It actually pushed Japan a few metres east, and made the local coastline subside by half a metre. It inundated 560 square kilometres of land, and killed 19,000 people immediately, as well as destroying partially or completely over a million buildings. Though this was catastrophic enough, the effect the earthquake and tsunami had on the Fukushima 1 Nuclear Power Plant was in many ways worse. In effect, the tsunami destroyed the generators needed to keep the reactors cool. This in turn meant that, after a day or so, they began to overheat, which led to meltdowns and potentially disastrous build-up of hazardous gases, which had to be released into the atmosphere, necessitating the evacuation of 10,000 inhabitants from the area.

It is hard to understand the implications of such an event, and perhaps many of us do not try to do so. In some ways, such an understanding can only be attempted through the most radical kind of thinking. In 2014, the French philosopher Jean-Luc Nancy was invited to Japan to discuss the implications of Fukushima. He suggested that 'to philosophize after Fukushima', the 'mandate I was given for this conference... inevitably makes me think of Adorno's: "To write poetry after Auschwitz is barbaric".'[11] For Nancy, Fukushima not only invokes Auschwitz but, as he puts it, 'the name of Fukushima... is accompanied by the sinister privilege that makes it rhyme with Hiroshima.'[12] According to Nancy, 'it is not possible to ignore what is suggested by the rhyme of these two names, for this rhyme gathers together—reluctantly and against all poetry—the ferment of something shared. It is a question—and since March 11, 2011, we have not stopped chewing on this bitter pill—of nuclear energy itself'.[13]

After Fukushima, Basho came to Hiraizumi, where he wrote one of his most famous haiku. Hiraizumi was (and indeed remains) famous as the place where the Fujiwara family built the Chūson-ji temple complex, which, in the words of the temple's official website, was intended to 'placate the spirits of those who had died, either friend or foe, in the bitter conflicts that had dominated Tohoku in the latter half of the late eleventh century', and to be 'a peaceful state' based on the principles of Pure Land Buddhism. To put it in context, Basho writes about the glory of generations of Fujiwaras passing away as if in a dream, leaving the ruins reduced to rice paddies. Even though, during those generations, there were many acts of chivalry, all those responsible for such deeds are dead and gone, leaving only a ruined castle on which only grass thrives, a fact that makes him weep, and inspires the haiku in question.

A thicket of summer grass
Is all that remains
Of the dreams and ambitions
Of ancient warriors.[14]

The Irish poet Derek Mahon was greatly influenced by Basho, and owned a treasured copy of *The Narrow Road to the Deep North*. Basho is the protagonist in Mahon's poem 'The Snow Party', which resembles a series of linked haiku.

Bashō, coming
To the city of Nagoya,
Is asked to a snow party.

There is a tinkling of china
And tea into china;
There are introductions.

Then everyone
Crowds to the window
To watch the falling snow.

Snow is falling on Nagoya
And farther south
On the tiles of Kyōto.

Eastward, beyond Irago,
It is falling
Like leaves on the cold sea.

Elsewhere they are burning
Witches and heretics
In the boiling squares,

Thousands have died since dawn
In the service
Of barbarous kings;

But there is silence
In the houses of Nagoya
And the hills of Ise.[15]

As Irene de Angelis has pointed out, 'The Snow Party' appears to have been developed out of an earlier unfinished poetic sequence inspired by John Hershey's book on Hiroshima, in which Basho's 'grieving ghost' is invoked.[16] De Angelis shows how some of the lines in Mahon's poem seem to be directly prefigured by notes he took from Hershey's book, such as 'everyone crowds to the window', and 'there is a tinkling of china'.[17] However, it seems as if Mahon cannot write poetry directly about Hiroshima. Perhaps to do so is also barbaric, as Adorno suggested about Auschwitz.

The Fukushima Nuclear Disaster is one of only two nuclear incidents to be given a rating of seven out of seven on the International Nuclear Events (INES) Scale, the other being Chernobyl in 1986 (and reading Svetlana Alexievich's book on Chernobyl leaves no doubt about the degree of disaster it represented). The INES scale has eight ratings, from zero, deviation, to seven, major accident. Only one event has been given a rating of six, the first recorded nuclear accident, which occurred in Mayak, Kyshtym, in Russia, in 1957. Five incidents have been rated at five, 'accident with wider consequences', which include the partial meltdown at Three Mile Meltdown, but also the second major nuclear accident after Mayak, the Windscale fire in Cumbria in October 1957. Perhaps more shockingly, Sellafield, the name now given to the whole complex in Cumbria which included Windscale, also achieved an incident rating of four, 'accident with local consequences', five times between 1955 and 1979. In 1957, the no. 1 pile of the Windscale 2-pile facility caught fire. This was nearly a far greater disaster than it turned out to be, and it helped foment considerable opposition to nuclear energy, as well as making Windscale one of those names that need little or no explanation (at least in Britain and Ireland).

The fact that the North West of England is not an uninhabited wasteland is down to the calm and intelligent response of Thomas Tuohy, general manager of Windscale in 1957. His decision to shut down the airflow to the reactor to quench the fire prevented a possible explosion and the far wider spread of radioactive materials. Without him, the fire at Windscale may have been as great a catastrophe as the meltdown at Chernobyl.

After visiting the Japanese garden, I drive back to the A595 and turn off towards Seascale, a small town on the sea, and, having parked, walk up the beach. Seascale was once a thriving resort, though this is hard to believe visiting it now. It was in Seascale in 1889 that the great Victorian art critic John Ruskin made his final journey outside Brantwood, the house he owned in the Lake District. He had just finished what would turn out to be his last piece of writing, the ending of *Praeterita*, his autobiography. By this time, his hand shook too much for him to be able to write, so he dictated the last parts of the book to his cousin Joan Severn. Severn decided that Ruskin should have a holiday, and took him and his friend and amanuensis W. G. Collingwood to Seascale, which Ruskin apparently already disliked, and where he found himself confused and unable to do any work. They returned earlier than planned, and an eyewitness account from the stationmaster at Coniston Railway Station attested to how old and tired Ruskin appeared on what would be his last train journey. As Tim Hilton puts it in his life of Ruskin: 'In the decade of life that remained to him, Ruskin would scarcely stir from his house and the Brantwood grounds'.[18]

It was during this stay at Seascale that Ruskin also made his last painting, a watercolour of the sun setting over the sea. Given that the sea is on the left of the picture, he must have been facing north, towards the place where the Sellafield Nuclear Power Station would be built some decades after his visit. Seascale never really prospered as a resort, and there is not much else to see, as attested in Pevsner, a fact celebrated by a short poem by the American poet Jonathan Williams (more about whom later).

Professor Pevsner
Unbowed by Culinary Deprivation
Stands on the Cumbrian Shore at Seascale:
'On the front
there is nothing to report.'[19]

On the day I visit, though clouds have built up, it is a still a beautiful day, and the sun breaks out of the clouds to pick out the mixture of sand and rock that make up the beach and to turn the sea a luminous blue. From Seascale, I can already see the towers of Sellafield. There is something strange about the juxtaposition of the normality of the scene, with people walking dogs on the beach. Yet, a few hundred metres up the coast there is a massive accumulation of highly radioactive materials. There is a footpath that runs right up the side of the complex, from which the trains that carry nuclear waste can be seen. The tracks and the highly protected gates which they go through to the plant remind me of the perimeter in

Tarkovsky's *Stalker*, through which the stalker and his companions must enter the Zone. In an article in *The Guardian* in 2009, Building B30 at Sellafield was described by the deputy managing director of the site as 'the most hazardous industrial building in Europe.' He went on to describe Building B38 as 'the second most hazardous industrial building in Europe.' The article describes how in B30 'piles of old nuclear reactor parts and decaying fuel rods, much of them of unknown provenance and age, line the murky, radioactive waters of the cooling pond in the centre of B30. Down there, pieces of contaminated metal have dissolved into sludge that emits heavy and potentially lethal doses of radiation.'[20]

B38 is where the cladding and fuel were 'simply thrown' and 'left to disintegrate' during the Miners' Strike of 1972, when plants such as Sellafield were run at full stretch and it proved impossible to process all the waste. Meanwhile, Building B41 still stores the aluminium cladding for the uranium fuel rods that were burnt in 1957, while Building B29 is a 'huge covered cooling pond that once stretched between the heat stacks of Piles 1 and 2.' As the article puts it:

Nuclear waste was tipped in at the top of B41 once it was erected and then allowed to fall to the bottom. Later, when it was realised that pieces of aluminium and magnesium among this waste could catch fire and cause widespread contamination, inert argon gas had to be pumped in to smother potential blazes.

Thus 'for the past 60 years, building B41 has remained in this state, its highly radioactive contents mingling and reacting with each other.'[21] It is for these reasons that Greenpeace describes Sellafield as a 'slow motion Chernobyl.'[22] A more recent report from 2015 in *The New Scientist* suggests that matters are no better now.

It must be said that nuclear power stations are much safer now. Recently, a colleague and I were given a 'writers' tour' around Heysham Nuclear Power Station, down the coast from Sellafield, just outside Morecambe. This visit offered a number of insights into nuclear power, one of which was that a nuclear power station is really little more than a massive kettle, and the sole purpose of the massive and potentially dangerous fission process at its heart is to heat millions of gallons of water to drive enormous turbines, which then turn a device that generates electricity based on the electromagnetic principles discovered by Michael Faraday in the 1830s. For all the mystique of nuclear power and the complexities of its operations, the basic idea is almost banally simple. It's exactly the same setup as a coal or water power station, with the proviso that, in this case, the power source is potentially incredibly dangerous. It is unsurprising therefore that the signage and, indeed, the whole interior environment of Heysham, evinced an obsessive concern with safety. From the moment a visitor approaches the site, he or she is confronted by endless signs informing anyone not aware of it that they are about to enter a controlled nuclear site, where specific laws and rules are in force. The United Kingdom has a specialist armed police service for guarding nuclear installations and nuclear materials in transit, the Civil Nuclear Constabulary, the motto of which is 'deter, defend, deny, recover'. Given understandable concerns about nuclear terrorism, the fact that the CNC is heavily armed is emphasised in any publicity. I felt perfectly safe in the station, despite being feet away from what is effectively a controlled nuclear explosion. The exterior of the station reminded me most strongly of the U.S.-Mexican border between San Diego and Tijuana which my daughter, sister and I had crossed a year or so earlier, with double sets of chain-linked fences, copious amounts of razor wire and heavily armed police. For my colleague, who had been a prison librarian, the interior of the station was exactly like a prison, particularly in relation to the various gates through which one might or might not be allowed to enter. We, of course, were massively restricted in terms of where we could go, and were only able to look at the reactors or the control room from special, glassed-in viewing platforms.

The only point at which this sense of safety was diminished was in relation to the trains taking the nuclear waste out of the station. As in Sellafield, the train line ran between chain-linked fences surmounted by razor wire. In the visitors' centre, we were shown a film of one of the metal containers in which the nuclear waste is stored for transportation being smashed into by a train, as a test. The train was almost entirely destroyed, while the container survived more or less intact, and now sits, slightly dented, outside one of the buildings at Heysham. The reassurance this was supposed to give was somewhat tempered by the knowledge that trains carrying nuclear waste in these containers were continually travelling from all over Britain to the one place where such waste can be stored until a proper, permanent solution to its storage can be devised, which is, of course, Sellafield. I once saw one of these trains pass as I sat in the Leighton Moss nature reserve near Silverdale at dusk. It was an eerie juxtaposition.

In his brilliant piece of poetic reportage *About a Mountain*, John D'Agata describes the complex and contradictory politics of nuclear waste storage in the United States, in particular in relation to the proposed storing of such waste in the Yucca Mountain project, in Nevada, a hundred miles from Las Vegas. This project, initiated in 1987, and, after considerable controversy, terminated by President Obama in 2011, reveals for D'Agata much of the sheer inhuman incomprehensibility of nuclear energy. For example, the project sets a timescale for the storage of nuclear waste of ten thousand years. D'Agata sets out to find how this particular figure was arrived at. In the end he discovers that it is, in the words of one of the scientists he interviews, fundamentally rhetorical or theatrical, echoing Derrida's description of nuclear war as 'fabulously textual'.[23] Ten thousand years may sound a long time in human terms but is next to meaningless in relation to the tens of millions of years during which nuclear waste is deadly. But even to make the apparently solid geology of Yucca Mountain safe for decades, let alone tens of thousands of years, seems extraordinarily difficult.[24] Beyond the question of physical security, there is also the problem of how to prevent people from entering the site, unaware of its lethal contents. In a bravura passage, D'Agata sketches out the condition of humanity ten thousand years ago, consisting of a total population of five million living a life in almost every way different to ours now. More pressingly, he shows how even language of five hundred years ago is more or less incomprehensible to a modern reader. Thus, the question of what kind of sign can continue to communicate danger for ten thousand years or even a thousand, let alone tens of millions, is almost impossible to answer. However, a commission was set up, consisting of geologists, engineers, linguists, astronomers, an artist and others thought capable of providing an answer. In a telling and resonant passage in the committee's report, the solution involved the very question of meaning itself, or, rather, its lack. As D'Agata points out, humans have always wanted to mark out the space that they have wanted to call 'the center'. This 'is an impulse to create order out of the chaos that surrounds us: the tribal fire, the village temple, the city's clock tower'. Thus, it is necessary to 'invert the symbolic logic of this site, establish a sense of meaningless around the entire mountain, suggest that there is no single place of value at the site... the land itself is shunned... devastated by the Earth'.[25] This is a bit like a malign version of Barthes' 'sacred nothing' he finds in the centre of Tokyo.

Windscale's first and prime use was not for energy but for weaponry. Calder Hall, which became operational in 1956 on the same site, was the energy generation unit. Windscale and Calder Hall were incorporated under the name Sellafield in 1981. From its inception as a nuclear facility in 1947, Windscale was the main producer of the plutonium needed for Britain's burgeoning nuclear weaponry project. In fact, it has been suggested that the Windscale fire was caused by the large amount of fissile material needed for Operation Grapple, the United Kingdom's hydrogen bomb project, and the various bombs it developed. As was the case with similar American devices, such bombs were tested in remote parts of the Pacific. Pretty much all such tests were filmed, and many can be viewed online. In the 1970s, before such accessibility, the artist Bruce Conner had got hold of and edited together footage from the 1946 Crossroads Tests at Bikini Atoll. The resulting film, *Crossroads*, in which he slows down the explosions, and sets them to a soundtrack of both electronic noise, and music by Terry Riley, is one of the most extraordinary, terrifying, and also beautiful, films I have seen, which seems to push at the very limits of what can be represented. As Adrian Searle, reviewing *Crossroads* in *The Guardian*, commented: 'Language has its limits. Words fail, and feel almost entirely inadequate when faced with such enormity'.[26] In fact, atomic and nuclear weapons presented enormous problems of language from the beginning. As William Shurcliff explains in *Bombs at Bikini*, the official report on the tests, one of the reasons observers 'had so much trouble in retaining a clear impression of the explosion phenomena was the lack of appropriate words and concepts. The explosion phenomena abounded in absolutely unprecedented inventions in solid geometry. No adequate vocabulary existed for these novelties'. Finally, 'after two months of verbal groping, a conference was held and over thirty special terms, with carefully drawn definitions, were agreed on'. These included dome, fillet, side jets, bright tracks, cauliflower cloud, fallout, air shock disk, water shock disk, base surge, water mound, uprush, after cloud.[27]

In his essay 'The Atomic Sublime', Peter Hales suggests that the mushroom cloud 'arrived as something close to what Roland Barthes has called a "pure sign"—a visual icon so unprecedented that, for a moment at least, it lay outside the webs of signification that comprised a watching culture'.[28] The early descriptions of the blasts struggle to find language adequate to what has been witnessed, though, according to Hales, they share an emphasis on natural imagery. For Hales, this represents a Romantic vision of atomic blasts as sublime, the atomic sublime.[29]

On the way home I went to Barrow-in-Furness, a town rarely visited by visitors to the Lakes, but which contains at least one extraordinary sight worth seeing. Barrow is a company town, originally for the shipbuilding and munitions company Vickers. Vickers was swallowed up in a complex series of nationalisations, mergers and acquisitions which produced the company known as BAE Systems. Among the many items of military and civilian hardware the company produces are the nuclear submarines of the British Navy, those which carry the Trident nuclear deterrent. In order to manufacture these vessels, the company constructed a vast complex known as the Devonshire Dock Hall. Designed to both optimise the process of construction and shield the submarines from espionage, it was built during the premiership of Margaret Thatcher, and is known locally as 'Maggie's Farm'. It is vast and dominates the town, but is also entirely opaque, in that nothing about it tells you anything about what goes on inside. In Barrow, I came across a pub in the centre of town named the Buddha Bar. Peter Sloterdijk claims that the atomic bomb is the 'real Buddha of the Western countries, a sovereign device, autonomous, perfect'.[30] Just down the road, at Conishead Priory, is the first Kadampa Temple for World Peace, which houses the largest bronze statue of Buddha cast in the West. Perhaps the juxtaposition of the Buddha with the Trident submarines at Barrow and the nuclear sites of Sellafield is less incongruous than it might seem.

All day the light has been something like a pure emptiness, a luminous emptiness. This last phrase I connect with Buddhism. It turns out to be the title of a book about the *Tibetan Book of the Dead*. It also reminds me of something I read about Tibetan religion. According to Guiseppe Tucci, all religion in the region, from Bon to Buddhism, is characterised by what he calls 'photism', which he defines as 'the great importance attached to light, whether as a generative principle, as a symbol of supreme reality, or as a visible, perceptible manifestation of that reality; light from which all comes forth and which is present within ourselves'.[31]

It reminds me of Jacques Derrida's description of the light worshipped in early religions according to Hegel, as pure light, simple determinability, pure medium, ethereal transparence in which nothing appears but the appearing, the pure light of the sun. This light is 'pure and figureless' and 'burns all. It burns itself in the all burning [*le brûle-tout*] it is, leaves, of itself or anything, no trace, no mark, no sign of passage.'[32] 'All burning' and '*brûle-tout*' are, of course, translations of 'holocaust'.

Thus I heard. On one occasion the Blessed One was living at Gaya, at Gayasisa, together with a thousand bhikkhus. There he addressed the bhikkhus.

Bhikkhus, all is burning. And what is the all that is burning?

The eye is burning, forms are burning, eye-consciousness is burning, eye-contact is burning, also whatever is felt as pleasant or painful or neither-painful-nor-pleasant that arises with eye-contact for its indispensable condition, that too is burning. Burning with what? Burning with the fire of lust, with the fire of hate, with the fire of delusion. I say it is burning with birth, aging and death, with sorrows, with lamentations, with pains, with griefs, with despairs.

The ear is burning, sounds are burning...
The nose is burning, odors are burning...
The tongue is burning, flavors are burning...
The body is burning, tangibles are burning...[33]

Bewcastle

One day, my friend Charlotte tells me about the Anglo-Saxon cross at Bewcastle, near Carlisle, one of the most spectacular monuments in the North West from its period, equalled only by the one in Ruthwell in Dumfriesshire, on the other side of the Solway Firth. I decide to go there on a rainy day in July. On the way, I plan a number of stops at sites that bear some relation to the cross.

I start the journey on the M6, passing the hills known as the Howgills, and then Tebay. This is the most spectacular section of the road, and possibly the most beautiful motorway experience in England as it passes through the Lune Gorge. The road curves round the hills, which resemble reclining human bodies, fleshy and curvaceous. After the theatre of the Howgills, the journey is less dramatic. Past Tebay, the landscape flattens out, though there is some drama in the knowledge that this section running over Shap Fell is one of the highest bits of motorway in England. The presence of windsocks indicates that this can be a perilous drive in high winds. At this point on the left, one of my favourite buildings in Cumbria comes into view, the Shapfell quarry. The most visible part of this is a complex arrangement of steel drums, girders and chimneys, from which thick, white smoke issues. The quarry, which is currently owned by Tata Steel, has been operating since 1962, and is mainly concerned with the production of quicklime and limestone products for the steel industry. The building is massively incongruous in relation to the Lake District, and could be straight from a photograph by Bernd and Hilla Becher, the great German photographers of industrial architecture. About a mile or so directly west from the quarry, on the side of the Wet Sleddale Valley, is Sleddale Hall, Uncle Monty's Crow Crag in *Withnail and*

I. The quarry is starkly visible from the house, though the film is careful not to show this, in order to preserve the romantic image of the countryside against which it sets the behaviour of the decadent southerners.

Beyond Tebay, the northbound and southbound carriages of the motorway bifurcate, with the southbound rising higher. Between the two there is a long stretch of rather forlorn and austere farmland, sometimes populated with livestock. This acts as a reminder that where I am travelling was once a remote and inaccessible valley, and that the motorway is an imposition on its particular ecology (though it's not quite as dislocating as the similar section of the M62 from Manchester to Leeds in which the farmland between the carriageways contains a deserted farmhouse).

For many years, the Lune Valley, rather than the Lune Gorge, was a possible site for the M6 motorway. The idea that a motorway could have been built through the narrow, and ecologically rich, environment of the valley seemed at first hard to countenance. Yet, in engineering terms, to route the road through the comparatively sheltered Lune Valley made sense, especially given the harsh, windswept conditions of the A6 at the Shap Saddle. In the 1950s the route was surveyed and planned, and it was halted only when a protest meeting was held in Kirkby Lonsdale in 1959, which pleaded the government to rethink. They commissioned Scott Wilson Kirkpatrick & Partners to look at all the alternatives. In the end, what was called the Killington Route through the Lune Gorge was chosen, and a set of complex solutions to its environmental difficulties resulted in the motorway being extended from Lancaster to Penrith by 1970.

The knowledge that the M6 might have been routed through the Lune Valley makes the experience of its current route more interesting. At one level it brings to mind Martin Heidegger's claim about the hydroelectric dam on the river Rhine, which turns it into 'standing reserve'.[1] By bisecting a once unified valley, and making its main purpose to be a travel corridor, the M6 reduces it, much as the river for Heidegger is reduced from a source of poetic and cultural meaning to a water power supplier. Driving through the stretch of the motorway from the Kirkby Lonsdale junction to the Tebay Junction is to be offered a kind of double vision. It is possible to mentally blot the road out of one's mind and to see the valley as it once was, remote, quiet and inaccessible. There is a strange scene in Nicholas Roeg's film *The Man Who Fell to Earth*, in which the limousine Thomas Jerome Newton (the alien played by David Bowie) is travelling in is suddenly transported in time to the early nineteenth century of American settlers, who look bemused as this apparition from the future appears in their midst. I can imagine something like that happening when I drive on this stretch of the M6. My car will suddenly find itself bouncing on the turf of a field in the valley's middle, rather than gliding on the motorway tarmac.

Just below Carlisle, I leave the motorway and make my way to my first stop, the small village of Wreay (pronounced 'rear'). I have decided to stop there because it contains one of the most remarkable buildings in Cumbria, St Mary's Church. My immediate impression is that it is not that unusual, though the more I look the more I see that it is not at all like other churches in the region, or indeed anywhere in the country. Designed and built by the extraordinary architect, antiquary and visionary Sarah Losh, between 1840 and 1842, it is based on the Roman basilicas of the early church, rather than on later Gothic edifices, the style of which was then being revived by Pugin and others. The apse is semi-circular, while the nave is rectangular. I particularly like St Mary's because it evinces a wonderfully proto-ecological sensibility on the part of Losh. Throughout the interior and exterior are unusual natural motifs, carved flowers in the font, marble pine cone finials.

The pine cone is both ubiquitous in and around the church and a poignant memorial of what must be a lost love. In the plot of land in which the mausoleum is sited there is a pine tree, and on the wall next to it, a giant pine cone, carved in stone, below which is the following inscription.

This Khelat Pine is planted in memory of Wm. Thain, Major of the 33rd, and was raised by seed transmitted by him to England. He perished in the fatal pass of Coord Cabal, esteemed and lamented by all who knew him.

It is for its connection to Thain and in memorial of his untimely death that the cone became such an emblem for Losh. In his book on Wreay, A. R. Hall describes how:

Cones terminate the dripstones over the west door of the Church which she built, and appear in the carvings of the windows above it. The door lock is carved in the shape of two cones. The nave is entered between two large cones of alabaster, a cone forms the centre ornament of each of the large beams of the roof, and a cone is also carved on the gravestone which covers both her sister and herself.[2]

Hall suggests that the cone was important for Losh, not just because of its connection to Thain, 'but as an emblem of life preserved through apparent death'.[3]

I enter the church through a semi-circular doorway, surrounded by carvings of water-lily leaves and flowers, terminated by cones. Above the door are three windows, each bordered with carvings, a chrysalis, with six butterflies and garlands of poppy-heads and wheat. The left-hand window has images of fossil ammonites, nautilus, sea-weeds and sea anemones, all creatures of the sea; the right-hand window shows creatures of air, raven, owl, cockchafer and bee, and branches of fir trees beating pine cones, and the middle window has fruits and flowers of the earth. The font is made of alabaster with ten panels, showing a dove with an olive leaf in its mouth, a dragonfly, ears of corn, a butterfly, lilies, lotus flowers and leaves, a pine tree, pomegranate, melon, a vine with grapes. On the font cover, of silvered glass, are alabaster lotus leaves and flowers. The lotus leaf motif is repeated in the alabaster altar candlesticks.

In her book on Sarah Losh and the church, Jenny Uglow claims that Losh 'decorated the church with symbols that looked back to the earlier religions, myths and cults, as the wheat of Demeter and the grapes of Dionysius lay behind the bread and wine of the sacrament'. The motif of the lotus, found all over the church, is 'one of the earliest symbols of creation'. I am fascinated to read how Uglow connects this to a distinctly pagan religiosity. She invokes the myths of the Nile that 'told that before the universe existed there was only an infinite ocean, the primeval being, Nun. Out of Nun a lotus flower arose on a patch of dry land and as the blossoms opened a child stepped out, the self-created sun god Atun or Ra. The lotus was the womb of earth and light, its petals closing at sunset. The lotus was the womb of earth and light, its petals closing at sunset and opening at dawn'.[4]

Uglow suggests that Losh knew that the lotus, whose flowers are 'untouched by the water around it or the mud from which it grew, represented detachment from worldliness'. It was, for Losh and the Romantics, a 'symbol of light, its petals representing the rays of the sun, and also of receptivity, reproduction and continuing life'.[5] Uglow looks to the Romantic reception of Hindu mythology as the source of this imagery, in particular in Robert Southey's poem 'The Curse of Kehama', which was influenced by Sir William Jones' translations of Sanskrit texts. Other influential writers on ancient religions of the time included Max Müller, Friedrich Kreuzer and Richard Payne Knight. Perhaps most important for Losh's church and its symbolism was Knight's *Inquiry into the Symbolical Language of Ancient Art and Mythology*, first published in 1818, with a new edition coming out in 1836, as she was planning the church's construction. Uglow does not know if Losh read the book but her chapel is full of symbols that Payne Knight mentions, 'from the cockerel, snake and tortoise... to the lotus and the pomegranate'.[6] According to Payne Knight, the 'lotus, pomegranate and barley corn... were emblems of female "passive generative power". Their counterpart, the "male, or active generative attribute", was the pinecone', found as a token of reproduction in Assyrian, Babylonian, Egyptian, Greek, Roman and even Christian religious imagery. The pine cone is also part of Masonic symbolism, referring to Descartes' siting of the spirit in the pineal gland.[7]

In the middle of the churchyard there is a nineteenth-century replica of the Bewcastle Cross. Losh and her sister had visited the Cross in the early part of the century, and had vowed to make a replica as a monument to their parents. Also in the churchyard there is a mausoleum built of rough stone, in which a number of marble medallions of family members are to be found, as well as a marble statue of Sarah Losh's younger sister Katherine, made by David Dunbar of Carlisle, with the following inscription.

Catherina Isabella, soror placens,
amabilis piaque: semper mihi carissima
eris: cara nunc tua pallida imago.

Hall translates this as 'Catherine Isabella, sweet, lovely, sisterly sister; always wilt though be most dear to me; dear too now is thy pale lifeless image'.[8] I love the spectrality of the last line.

Next stop on my journey is Brampton, to revisit St Martin's Church, notable for being designed by the Pre-Raphaelite associate Philip Webb, his only church, and having stained glass by Edward Burne Jones and William Morris. The glass in particular is ravishing. The east window behind the altar, with its three rows of figures, illuminates the church in a way that most other stained glass simply fails to do. The church was built for George Howard, ninth Earl of Carlisle, a fascinating figure in his own right. Howard appears to have been unlike many of his aristocratic contemporaries, despite being educated at Eton and Cambridge. After university he studied art, and went on to be a painter of some repute.

He also commissioned a house from Webb in the Arts and Crafts style. His granddaughter Winifred Roberts became a celebrated artist, better known as Winifred Nicholson, after her marriage to the painter Ben Nicholson.

After Brampton, I make my way to Lanercost Priory, one of the many ruined abbeys and monasteries that are found in the North of England. The priory itself is half a ruin of the old monastery and half a functional church. The former is run by English Heritage, and you enter through a gift shop. It is smaller than the great monasteries of Yorkshire such as Rievaulx or Fountains, and darker, being made out of the red sandstone common in this part of the North. Its size and darkness perhaps make it more romantic than larger such remains. It is reminiscent of those paintings by Caspar David Friedrich of monks filing into snowbound ruins, or of the Abbey of San Galgano in Italy, memorably used by Andrei Tarkovsky in his film *Nostalghia* (and which I remember breaking into with another friend named Charlotte in the 1980s). The abbey has a number of tombs, some of which are for members of the Howard family and date from the nineteenth and twentieth centuries.

Leaving Lanercost, I am uncertain how to get to Bewcastle, the next and final stop on this journey. I find myself going along the old military road that follows Hadrian's Wall, past both Banks Head, where Winifred Nicholson lived most of her life, and Banks, the house rented by the Chinese artist Li Yuan-chia, whom Nicholson befriended. Li Yuan-chia was an extraordinary character, who was one of the first Chinese abstract painters, as a member of the Taiwanese Ton Fan movement. In the early sixties he moved to Bologna, and then to London, at the invitation of David Medalla, and showed at the Lisson Gallery. At the end of the decade he moved to what was then known as Cumberland, and bought a derelict farmhouse on Hadrian's Wall from Nicholson. In 1972 he established the LYC Museum there, in which he showed a number of internationally famous artists. In 1983, after ten years of operation, the museum closed. At this point, he tried to sell part of the building to an unscrupulous buyer, who ended up as a sitting tenant, refusing to either move out or buy what he had promised, and who tied Li Yuan-chia up in litigation for several years. He died of intestinal cancer in 1994 and is buried in the graveyard at Lanercost Priory.

The building that housed the LYC Museum has not been lived in or used since, and the windows still have traces of the name. The LYC is on the Roman road that runs alongside Hadrian's Wall, and I realise that this means I am going east, rather than north, as I should be, so I turn round and take a road I guess is going in the right direction. This turns out to be correct, though Bewcastle is still another seven or eight miles further north, along a narrow, empty road. Bewcastle was originally one of three outposts built by Emperor Hadrian, as part of the forward defences of his eponymous wall. Even in a car in the twenty-first century it feels remote. It is hard to imagine what it must have felt like in Hadrian's time for a legionary, a good two to three hours' march at least away from the wall that divided Roman civilisation from barbarity.

Running between the Solway Firth and Newcastle, the Wall was Emperor Hadrian's attempt to put limits on the expansion of the Roman Empire and to consolidate its borders. The landscape through which the Wall runs is bare and harsh. The North has always been a site of mystery, a place of haunting and death. Despite it being sixteen hundred years since the end of the Roman occupation, the North West still has a sense of being at the end of empire, a marginal part of a marginal province. Provincial derives from *provincia*, the term used in the Roman Empire to denote those administrative areas outside Italy. Britannia was of course one such *provincia*, though this did not properly extend to encompass the whole of what we now think of as Britain. Indeed, what is now North West England was the limit of the Roman occupation, and also the furthest reach of empire, the greatest distance from Rome.

Some 80 feet south of the Wall, near Carrawburgh, there are the remains of a temple of Mithras or 'Mithraeum'. The cult of Mithras, the origins of which may lie in Iran and the Manichean religion of Mithra, flourished between the first and fourth centuries of the Common Era, and as a male-only affair, strongly appealed to the military. As a secret mystery cult, without either public visibility or existing writings, practically nothing is known about it. There are practically no extant texts on its rites and beliefs. In particular, the story which is being represented on many of the reliefs in the Mithraea is entirely mysterious. This absence may well have resulted from the silence that initiates were bound to keep about what they experienced. What Walter Burkett calls the 'fundamental event' of the Mithraic myth is clearly Mithras slaying a bull.[9] The reliefs that show this scene, one of which was found near Hadrian's Wall, are remarkable for how similar they are, especially in terms of following a specific iconography. The standard Mithraic image of the so-called Tauroctony shows Mithras in a cave, wearing Anatolian costume and wearing a Phrygian cap, astride a bull and pulling its head back from its muzzle rather than by its horn with his left hand while stabbing it in the neck with his other hand. Below the neck, catching the blood, are a dog and a snake. A scorpion is attacking the bull's genitals. Two torch bearers stand on either side, Cautes with his torch pointing up and Cautopates with his torch pointing down. Sol is on the upper left, and Luna on the upper right, possibly driving a chariot. Sometimes the scene is encircled by the signs of the Zodiac or other scenes from Mithras' life.

In the temple there are three dedicated alters (now replaced with reproductions with the originals in The Great North Museum in Newcastle). The centre alter has the following inscription: 'Deo Inv(icto) M(ithrae) L(ucius) Antonius Proculus praef(ectus) coh(ortis) I Bat(avorum) Antoninianae v(otum) s(olvit) l(ibens) m(erito)'. (To the Invincible god Mithras Lucius Antonius Proculus, prefect of the First Cohort of Batavians Antoniniana, willingly and deservedly fulfilled his vow). The one on the right, the east-ernmost, reads as follows: 'D(eo) In(victo) M(ithrae) s(acrum) Aul(us) Cluentius Habitus pra(e)f(ectus) coh(ortis) I Batavorum domu Ultin(i)a (tribu) Colon(ia) Sept(imia) Aur(elia) L(arino) v(otum) s(olvit) l(ibens) m(erito)'. (Sacred to the Invincible god Mithras: Aulus Cluentius Habitus, prefect of the First Cohort of Batavians, of the Ultinian voting-tribe, from Colonia Septimia Aurelia Larinum, willingly and deservedly fulfilled his vow.) The westernmost alter features a 'low relief' with 'the torso of Mithras facing front, with arms set at his waist as he rises from the rock. His cloak covers his body and left arm; in his right hand he holds a whip, which identifies him with Sol'.[10] Its inscription reads 'Deo Invicto Mitrae M(arcus) Simplicius Simplex pr(a)ef(ectus) v(otum) s(olvit) l(ibens) m(erito)'. (To the Invincible god Mithras Marcus Simplicius Simplex, prefect, willingly and deservedly fulfilled his vow.) These are the only records of these men, who have otherwise disappeared into historical oblivion. Yet, owing to the inscriptions they left, they are remembered. Their names are, literally, written in stone. It reminds me of a poem by Robinson Jeffers.

Stone-cutters fighting time with marble, you fore-defeated
Challengers of oblivion
Eat cynical earnings, knowing rock splits, records fall down,
The square-limbed Roman letters
Scale in the thaws, wear in the rain. The poet as well
Builds his monument mockingly:
For man will be blotted out, the blithe earth dies, the brave sun
Die blind, his heart blackening:
Yet stones have stood for a thousand years, and pained thoughts found
The honey peace in old poems.[11]

Perhaps every landscape can be seen inscribed by the endless passionate and violent processes through which it bears witness to what it has endured, whether meteorological, geological, biological or human, but it is the human inscription that binds such a landscape to language and thus to history and the human. By inscribing their names in the stone altarpieces these men mark the distinction between the human and the non-human. Carving the names, as an inscription, a trace of their presence, is paradigmatic of language.

The point of the border is the border itself, a kind of margin that delineates and defines the empire it encloses. Marginal comes from the proto-indo European *marǵ*, meaning 'border, boundary, or edge', and from which derive a number of cognate terms, including 'margin', but also 'march', and 'mark'. Here we can see a fruitful relation between the making of marks, as in writing, and the patrolling of boundaries and borders, marching. The area at the edge of Roman occupation, the Scottish border, is also known as the Scottish Marches, indicating the actions needed to secure this boundary. The Emperor Hadrian, in his drive to consolidate the Empire, and to set limits to its extent, made this notion of the marches literal in building the Wall. In fact, the remains of the Wall more often take the form of hollows scored into the land, scratched and inscribed into it, with earth pushed up on either side.

In this one can find a close relation between the making of marks, language and marching. To build a wall is to erect a boundary between inside and outside, between order and disorder, friend and enemy. Hadrian's Wall has been named, possibly anachronistically, as *Limes Britannicus*. *Limes*, plural *limites*, here is a Latin noun which can mean a number of things, including path, boundary line or marker, stream or indeed any marker of difference. (Here one can see a clear connection between this word and structuralist notions of language.) It is also cognate with *limen*, 'threshold', from whence we derive the word 'liminal'. According to a UNESCO website on the Roman borders, they 'were as much a mental barrier as material'. The *limes* was a 'sort of sacred border beyond which human beings did not transgress, and if they did, it was evidence that they had passed the bounds of reason and civilization. To cross the border was the mark of a savage.[12]

This part of the world is still the location of remote military establishments, firing ranges and so on. Among the most mysterious is RAF Spadeadam, about four miles north of Hadrian's Wall. It is a site of nearly 10,000 acres of forest and mire, dedicated to the testing of missiles and practising low flying for RAF and NATO forces. It was originally founded in the late 1950s as a base to test the Blue Streak, Britain's proposed Intermediate Range Ballistic Missile (IBRM). Before the establishment of the base, nothing happened there and it was known as the Spadeadam Waste.

Eventually I get to Bewcastle, and follow a sign pointing the way up a little hill to 'The Church and Cross'. The churchyard is surrounded by a low drystone wall, outside of which there is a transit van from whose interior hot tea and sandwiches are being dispensed to a group of fluorescent-clad cyclists, seemingly in their sixties and seventies. The church itself is small, and insignificant. It looks to date from the Georgian period, without being 'Georgian' in style. The front door leads to a panelled passage, with a staircase on the left up to a gallery.

By contrast with the modesty of church, the Cross is extraordinarily impressive, not least because it looks so out of place in this small churchyard. It reminds me of the monolith in the film *2001: A Space Odyssey*, so incongruous does it look among the eighteenth- and nineteenth-century gravestones. Little wonder that Pevsner describes it and the cross at Ruthwell as 'the greatest achievement of their date in the whole of Europe.'[13] Even without the cross head that must have sat on top of the shaft, it is fourteen foot high, tapering towards the top.

Like many such monuments it is enigmatic. The inscription on the west face, which might have indicated its purpose, is now more or less unreadable. What makes it so special, apart from its grandeur and comparative state of preservation, is the intricacy of the carving, and its beauty. The Cross began to be recorded in the works of various antiquarians such as William Camden, from the late sixteenth or early seventeenth century onwards. In the late nineteenth century, the artist W. G. Collingwood, amanuensis to John Ruskin, discussed the Cross in his work *Northumbrian Crosses of the Pre-Norman Age.*

Collingwood's interest in such crosses clearly influenced his design for John Ruskin's gravestone in Coniston (next to which he and his wife are buried). Ruskin died in 1900, and was buried in Coniston churchyard, at his request, rather than at Westminster Abbey, as many of his followers and admirers would have preferred. His grave is marked by a cross designed by Collingwood in imitation of Anglo-Saxon crosses found in the North such as that at Bewcastle. Among other notable features it includes what Collingwood describes as 'the ancient filfol or swastika, the revolving cross, supposed to have been at first a rude hieroglyph of the sun in its course, and thence a symbol of the rise of human life, – to the Christian church, which adopted the sign in the early ages, meaning also the sunrise of another day, resurrection to another life'.[14]

Collingwood's son, the philosopher and historian R. G. Collingwood, is buried next to his father and mother in the Coniston churchyard. The younger Collingwood built on his father's work on the Cross in a small pamphlet issued by the Cumberland and Westmorland Antiquarian and Archaeological Society in 1934. He was an extraordinary character, who was not only a highly influential philosopher, one of the now largely forgotten British Hegelian idealists, who became the Waynflete Professor of Metaphysical Philosophy at Oxford, but also spent his long vacations as an archaeologist, particularly round Hadrian's Wall and the north of England. He is perhaps best known for his philosophy of history, as expounded in a book published posthumously after his death at the early age of fifty-three. For Collingwood, history is, in the end, the study of what people thought, rather than the objective facts of their situation at any time. The historian's task is to try to imagine what a historical figure actually thought and why.

The cut, engraved nature of the Cross makes me think about the primacy of engraving, of scratching into a hard surface as something originary, and somehow bound up with the very fact of human culture. Bound up with this is the complex patterning, which also hints at some aspect of that culture, how it always involves intricate imbrication of lines meeting and crossing. That engraving is something primary, forceful, is found in Basil Bunting's great poem *Briggflatts*, which celebrates Bunting's love for Peggy, the stonemason's daughter.

The mason stirs:
Words!
Pens are too light
Take a chisel to write.[15]

Like both Collingwoods, Bunting was also a great admirer of the Northern art of which the Bewcastle Cross is an important example. For Bunting, such art was exemplified by the intricate design of the Lindisfarne Codex, which he had in mind as he worked on the equally intricate structure of *Briggflatts*. In an interview he describes the Codex as 'all interlacings of one sort or another. Nothing follows through without being crossed by something else.' For Bunting, this is analogous to, or even a 'parable' for, poetry. He points out how the best pages are those featuring the Cross, but that you have to look two or three times to see it. 'It's not in any way underlined. It emerges slowly out of this extremely complex design around it. There's no mistaking it. It is there, it does emerge, but it's not thrust at you.'[16]

This set of interests in the complex and labyrinthine nature of Northern, Celtic art and the originary primacy of engraving is shared by Ruskin. Engraving is the subject of one of Ruskin's most fascinating discourses, in *Ariadne Florentina*, his series of lectures on wood and metal engraving given at Oxford in 1872. As J. Hillis Miller has pointed out, this is far more than merely an account of its ostensible subject matter, but is perhaps something more like an equivalent to Martin Heidegger's essay on the origin of the work of art. Miller goes on to suggest that for Ruskin, that sign 'is always a miniature maze and is always connected to its context by labyrinthine lines of connection'.[17] As Jay Fellows and others have pointed out, Ruskin's thought was labyrinthine and he was fascinated by mazes and other figures, a fascination that explains the title of his lectures on engraving.[18] Perhaps here Ruskin prefigures the work of thinkers such as Derrida. The labyrinth is a key figure for Derrida, for whom language is always labyrinthine. 'The labyrinth... is an abyss: we plunge into the horizontality of a pure surface which itself represents itself from detour to detour'.[19]

Near the end of the last lecture, describing Botticelli's engraving of the Hellespontine Sybil Ruskin describes the lettering and suggests that in 'its weird characters, you have the best example I can show you of the orders of decorative design which are especially expressible by engraving, and which belong to a group of art instincts scarcely now to be understood, much less recovered, (the influence of modern naturalistic imitation being too strong to be conquered)—the instincts, namely, for the arrangement of pure line, in labyrinthine intricacy, through which the grace of order may give continual clue'. He continues that:

The entire body of ornamental design, connected with writing, in the Middle Ages seems as if it were a sensible symbol, to the eye and brain, of the methods of error and recovery, the minglings of crooked with straight, and perverse with progressive, which constitute the great problem of human morals and fate; and when I chose the title for the collected series of these lectures, I hoped to have justified it by careful analysis of the methods of labyrinthine ornament, which, made sacred by Theseian traditions, and beginning, in imitation of physical truth, with the spiral waves of the waters of Babylon as the Assyrian carved them, entangled in their returns the eyes of men, on Greek vase and Christian manuscript—till they closed in the arabesques which sprang round the last luxury of Venice and Rome.[20]

The section in *Ariadne* on wood engraving is itself a labyrinthine set of oppositions, between wood and metal, between the 'ditches filled with ink' of metal engraving and the 'ridges' rubbed with ink of wood engraving, between black and white and the complex differences about how they are handled in each technique, between thick and thin lines, between the experimentality of sketching and the decisiveness of engraving.[21] In a sense, Ruskin reduces all mark-making to pure difference, or even, given his trope of labyrinthine deferral, *différance*.

Engraving is, for Ruskin, something far more originary than merely making images, but seems to encompass the very things that distinguish us as humans, such as agriculture. Quoting a definition of engraving as meaning 'to decorate a surface with furrows', he suggests that 'a ploughed field is the purest type of such art; and is, on hilly land, an exquisite piece of decoration.'[22] Furthermore for Ruskin, what Miller calls 'the primordial material act of scratching a surface to make it a sign' encompasses both writing and drawing.[23]

The idea of scratching as some kind of originary technicity is alluded to in his description of the wood engraving tool, which 'is a solid ploughshare, which, instead of throwing the earth aside, throws it up and out, producing at first a simple ravine, or furrow, in the wood or metal, which you can widen by another cut, or extend by successive cuts'. He even includes an illustration of the tip of the tool, 'by which means the furrow produced is at first the wedge-shaped or cuneiform ravine', the word cuneiform here implicitly invoking scratching as also the first writing.[24]

By tracing both image-making and writing back to the scratch, Ruskin also anticipates Derrida's notion of the trace and of archiwriting, *archiécriture*. Thus, at least in his writing on wood engraving, Ruskin begins to appear like a proto-Grammatologist, and a thinker of originary technicity. In *Of Grammatology* Derrida suggests that:

It is a matter of writing by furrows. The furrow is the line, as the ploughman traces it: the road-*via rupta*-broken by the ploughshare. The furrow of agriculture, we remind ourselves, opens nature to culture (cultivation). And one also knows that writing is born with agriculture which happens only with sedentarization.[25]

For Derrida, the beginnings of what he calls 'civilized man' [*l'homme policé*] are bound up with the simultaneous development of agriculture in the form of ploughing and of the alphabet. Timothy Morton suggests that our current ecological catastrophe can be traced back to the very beginnings of agriculture, or what he calls 'agrilogistics'.[26] He quotes from both the Ramayana and Genesis to show that, in the former, agriculture represented a descent from the Golden Age, when it was an abomination, and in the latter, the outcome of the Fall of Man, who is condemned to 'struggle to scratch a living' from the earth. Given that settled cultivation is supposed to have started in Mesopotamia twelve thousand years ago, Morton names us 'mesopotamians'.[27]

In *Ariadne Fiorentina*, John Ruskin looks to marks made on rock and stone for his conception of the originary nature of writing. For Ruskin, the line is the 'simplest work of art you can produce', but he asks, 'what is the simplest means you can produce it with?' He points out that even a 'Cumberland lead pencil is a work of art in itself, quite a nineteenth century machine'. Thus, the simplest means to produce the simplest work of art is the scratch, so simple even kittens can do it. The scratch is 'the first and last of lines', and engraving is 'the art of scratch'.[28]

Contra Walter Benjamin, for Ruskin, engraving is not primarily about mechanical reproducibility but about permanence. It is, in his words, 'essentially the cutting into a solid substance for the sake of making your ideas as permanent as possible, graven with an iron pen in the Rock for ever. Permanence, you observe, is the object, not multiplicability; —that is quite an accidental, sometimes not even a desirable, attribute of engraving.'[29]

Ruskin makes the connection between engraving, writing and agriculture with death, especially with his choice of Holbein's engravings from the series 'The Dance of Death'. As Jonah Siegel points out, he puts the grave in engraving. Indeed, Ruskin uses the discussion about the Holbein engravings to work through an understanding of death itself. In his analysis of the engraving 'The Two Preachers', he shows how death reveals the ultimate hypocrisy of even the most sincere cleric. The other engraving, 'The Last Furrow', offers a 'more plain and more beautiful' message.

The husbandman is old and gaunt, and has past his days, not in speaking, but pressing the iron into the ground. And the payment for his life's work is, that he is clothed in rags, and his feet are bare on the clods; and he has no hat—but the brim of a hat only, and his long, unkempt grey hair comes through. But all the air is full of warmth and of peace; and, beyond his village church, there is, at last, light indeed. His horses lag in the furrow, and his own limbs totter and fail: but one comes to help him. 'It is a long field,' says Death; 'but we'll get to the end of it to-day,—you and I.'[30]

Here, it is hard not to hear an echo of Heidegger's famous account of the peasant woman in the field, from 'The Origin of the Work of Art'.

From out of the dark opening of the well-worn insides of the shoes the toil of the worker's tread stares forth. In the crudely solid heaviness of the shoes accumulates the tenacity of the slow trudge through the far-stretching and ever-uniform furrows of the field swept by a raw wind. On the leather lies the dampness and richness of the soil. Under the soles slides the loneliness of the field-path as evening falls. The shoes vibrate with the silent call of the earth, its silent gift of the ripening grain, its unexplained self-refusal in the wintry field. This equipment is pervaded by uncomplaining worry as to the certainty of bread, wordless joy at having once more withstood want, trembling before the impending birth, and shivering at the surrounding menace of death. This equipment belongs to the earth and finds protection in the world of the peasant woman. From out of this protected belonging the equipment itself rises to its resting-within-itself.[31]

Ruskin, like Heidegger, knows how life is made meaningful through death. According to Ruskin, '[E]ngraving means, primarily, making a permanent cut or furrow in something,' but 'The central syllable of the word has become a sorrowful one, meaning the most permanent of furrows.'[32] For Jonah Siegel, Ruskin understood the fear of death and the failure to see it as productive as a foundational error of modernity, and his lectures on engraving, like the Holbein prints he discusses, are memento mori that aim for a transvaluation of the power of the grave. As Siegel puts it, Ruskin sees 'Death as a limit or boundary adding significance to life, the carved line aiming at permanence by means of controlled, difficult work on hard material (stone, metal, wood) — these are elements that make the recuperation of the grave possible.'[33] Siegel sets the permanence of the grave and its capacity to offer rest against modernity's production of disposal, reproduced work.

In a footnote to his essay 'Force and Signification,' Derrida takes issue with Feuerbach's claim that 'the element of speech is air, the most spiritual and most universal vital medium.' Derrida suggests that 'air is not the element in which history develops if it does not rest [itself] on earth? Heavy, serious, solid earth. The earth that is worked upon, scratched, written upon. The no less universal medium in which meaning is engraved so that it will last.'[34]

The language Derrida uses in this passage is overdetermined linguistically. As Christopher Johnson points out, what is translated here as 'serious' is '*grave*' in French, which not only implies weightiness and heaviness, but also 'communicates' with graver, the word Derrida uses to denote inscription on the earth (and of course the grave in which we are buried). Johnson continues that 'Furthermore the hardness and heaviness of the earth presents a greater resistance to inscription than does the ethereal medium of speech'.[35] The earth has to be 'worked upon' or even 'scratched and clawed'. This is why later in the footnote Derrida suggests that 'Hegel would be of assistance here', suggesting, in Johnson's words, this 'presentation of inscription as passion and violence, difficulty and constraint'.[36]

In this, Ruskin anticipates the importance of being-towards-death in the work of Martin Heidegger. In his essay on the Bewcastle Cross and its relation to the place in which it is sited, Fred Orton invokes Heidegger, and in particular his notion of dwelling. For Orton, '[I]n front of the Bewcastle monument, sensing and making sense of "place", one must begin "thinking" about "dwelling" and about being-in-the-world'.[37] He quotes from Heidegger's essay 'Building Dwelling Thinking'.

Earth is the serving bearer, blossoming and fruiting, spreading out in rock and water, rising up into plant and animal. When we say earth, we are already thinking of the other three along with it, but we give no thought to the simple oneness of the four... The sky is the vaulting path of the sun, the course of the changing, moon, the wandering glitter of the stars, the year's seasons and their changes, the light and dusk of day, the gloom and glow of night, the clemency and inclemency of the weather, the drifting clouds and blue depth of the ether.... The divinities are the beckoning messengers of the godhead. Out of the holy sway of the godhead, the god appears in his presence or withdraws into his concealment.... The mortals are the human beings. They are called mortals because they can die. To die means to be capable of death as death. Only man dies, and indeed continually, as long as he remains on earth, under the sky, before the divinities.[38]

This is, Orton suggests, what 'the monument was intended to do: to situate those who used it in a fixed relation with it in such a way that, before it, they might glimpse something of the fundamental character of the being-in-the-world'.[39]

Looking at Google Maps before setting out I had noticed something called The Bewcastle House of Prayer on the edge of Bewcastle itself. I clicked on the link to the website and found that, as far as I could tell, it is a project to develop a kind of religious retreat combining ecotheology and permaculture, a set of agricultural techniques that are 'about living lightly on the planet, and making sure that we can sustain human activities for many generations to come, in harmony with nature. Permanence is not about everything staying the same. It's about stability, about deepening soils and cleaner water, thriving communities in self-reliant regions, biodiverse agriculture and social justice, peace and abundance'. According to its website, the House of Prayer is inspired by the proximity of the Cross and the kind of Christianity it supposedly represents; one, supposedly, based on Celtic and Saxon versions, which is more attuned to the earth and its needs. On the website, various introductions to their work and sermons or talks show them to be inspired by the presence of the Cross and its symbolism in establishing their community in Bewcastle. They also appear to be influenced by the great twentieth-century Orthodox theologian Sergei Bulgakov, who expounded what has been described as a 'religious materialism' appropriate for what Charles Taylor calls the 'immanent frame' of secularism.[40] It would seem their entire project is an attempt to redeem humankind from the fall into scratching the earth described in Genesis by using the techniques of permaculture. A note in one of their blog entries explains that:

'Civilised' societies have used the plough for thousands of years to break the ground, disrupt the growth of the indigenous vegetation, and provide a medium in which new seed can grow… ploughs require enormous amounts of energy to turn the earth. This destroys not only the plants already growing, but also the soil structure, developing 'plough pans' that inhibit the redevelopment of soil structure and create barriers to drainage'.[41]

When I find Greenholme, where the House of Prayer is supposedly located, it seems deserted and there is no evidence of any activity.

Boustead Hill

I travelled up the Cumbrian coast, past St Bees, past Whitehaven, Working and Maryport and onto Burgh Sands, on the edge of the Solway Firth that divides Cumbria from Scotland. It's a long journey to one of the remotest parts of Cumbria. A strange place, therefore, for aliens to visit. On 24 May 1964, on Burgh Sands, Carlisle fireman Jim Templeton took a photograph of his daughter. According to David Clarke and Andy Roberts' article in *The Fortean Times*,[1] when he collected the developed film the shop assistant said, 'That's a marvellous colour film, but who's the big fellow'. The photograph showed what appeared to be a figure wearing a space helmet standing behind his daughter. Templeton claimed to have no recollection of any such figure when he took the photograph. It was featured in the local press and became known around the world as the 'Solway Spaceman'. The Ministry of Defence only showed an interest when contacted by the *Cumberland News*. They offered to analyse the photograph, but Templeton refused to give them the film and camera. What happened next fuelled the speculative frenzy of UFOlogists. Clarke and Roberts describe how Jim was visited at the fire station by two men dressed entirely in black and driving a black Jaguar. They asked to be taken to where the photograph was taken. They showed Jim an identity card with an official crest and the word 'Security', and told him 'We're from the Ministry, but you don't need to know who we are. We go by numbers', referring to each other as 'nine' and 'eleven'. After Jim showed them where he had taken the photograph, they left, abandoning him to walk back to the fire station and he never saw them again.[2]

Perhaps most intriguingly for UFOlogists, 'Jim's photograph has been linked to an anomalous "figure" that was supposed to have appeared on a Blue Streak missile firing range at Woomera in south Australia. The link with Solway Firth was that Blue Streak missiles were developed and tested at RAF Spadeadam in Cumbria. They were part of a British missile system designed to be used as the first stage of a satellite launcher'.

The day after the photograph was taken, a Blue Streak launch had to be abandoned because 'because two large men [were] seen on the firing range... technicians at the time did not know about Templeton's sighting until it appeared on the front page of an Australian newspaper... and they said the figure in Cumbria looked the same as the ones they had seen on the monitor at Woomera'.[3] Templeton repeated this for a BBC interview, claiming that the Australian technicians at Woomera had said the figures were identical to that in the Solway Spaceman photograph.[4]

Of course, disappointingly perhaps, all the facts that might seem to suggest the actual presence of a genuine spaceman can be explained otherwise. The 'men in black' were probably hoaxers, or, as Clarke and Roberts put it, 'Walter Mitty types'.[5] The Blue Streak tests were abandoned, but for banally normal reasons. As for the photograph, the most convincing explanation is that Templeton's wife wandered into shot without him noticing, facing away from the camera when he actually took the shot. The viewfinder of the camera he was using only allowed him to see about 70% of what would appear in a photograph. The sunlight probably made her blue dress appear white, and the back of her head and brown hair are what look like the front of the spaceman's helmet. (Or at least that's what they want you to think.) However, the Solway Spaceman did help to revive the fortunes of British UFOlogy, which at the time was, in Clarke and Roberts' words, 'in the doldrums' and the 'great days of the 1950s saucer scares and contactees, when flying saucers made news headlines on a daily basis, were long gone and both flying saucer enthusiasts and media alike were looking for any story that would keep flying saucers in the public eye'. The Solway Spaceman photograph offered the opportunity for this and came just at about the time of British UFOlogy's great re-invention in 1966 when the so-called Warminster Phenomenon began, with a considerable number of UFO sightings over the Wiltshire town of Warminster from 1964 to the early 1970s.

Fascinatingly, British UFOlogy's first emergence was also due to a sighting in Cumbria. On 15 February 1954, thirteen-year-old Stephen Darbishire and his eight-year-old cousin Adrian Meyer went up the fell below the hill known as the Old Man of Coniston with a Box Brownie camera. Darbishire claimed that he knew 'absolutely nothing' about flying saucers. Apparently the youngster experienced 'a nagging persistent restlessness' that fateful morning, as if something was urging him that he must go up the hill behind his home; 'he could not tell why; he merely knew he had to.'[6]

According to his account, while on the Fell, Meyer pointed out something strange to Darbishire, something silvery and glassy, 'like aluminium in the sunlight', which approached them from Coniston, disappeared, reappeared and then hovered noiselessly within 400 yards of where Darbishire and Meyer were. In Darbishire's words to the local press:

The object was glistening and it was a silvery milky colour. You could tell the outline of it very plainly indeed and see port-holes along the upper part, and a thing which looked like a hatch on top. There were three bumps underneath and the centre of the underneath part was of a darker colour. I took the first picture when it was moving very slowly about three or four hundred yards away and then it disappeared from my view as there was some undergrowth in the way. When it came into sight again I took another picture but then it suddenly went up into the sky in a great swish. As it went upwards it tilted and I could see the underneath side more clearly. There was some sort of whistling sound as it went up which I think was the wind.[7]

The boys ran back to Darbishire's house where they reported what they had seen to his father, who made his son write a report and make a sketch of the object. What he drew looked remarkably like the flying saucers supposedly photographed by George Adamski, the founder of modern UFOlogy. Even more remarkable was that the camera film, when developed, also appeared to show a saucer-shaped object, in which, despite the fuzziness of the image, some of the details described by Darbishire could be seen. As with the later case of the Solway Spaceman, the local and then the national newspapers became involved and the word about Darbishire's sighting spread. The *Lancashire Evening Post* published the image next to that of the Venusian 'Scout Ship' taken by Adamski. Following this, Desmond Leslie, Irish aristocrat and co-author of a seminal text on UFOs with Adamski, travelled to Coniston to stay with the Darbishire family, and proclaimed the genuineness of the image. (I am fascinated to discover that Leslie was a pioneering composer of electronic music and musique concrete. Between 1955 and 1959 he produced a number of compositions from which he made a single acetate, entitled *Music of the Future*, which was used in, among other programmes, *Dr Who*.) Despite Darbishire's claim that he knew nothing about flying saucers, it is fairly obvious that he was aware of them, and had even seen the image of the Adamski saucer published in *Illustrated Magazine* in September 1953. Later, Darbishire would claim his photograph was faked, and then retract that claim, suggesting he had done so in order to discourage unwelcome attention.

In 2004, *The Westmoreland Gazette* reported that a Bristol-based artist, Julian Claxton, was going to 'head up the river valley footpath to Little Arrow Moor to recreate what is held to be the first UFO photograph ever taken in Britain.' Using a fishing rod, a wooden frame and a silvery shape, he intended to investigate the different ways that Darbishire may have made the image. According to the newspaper, 'well-known artist Mr Darbishire, now 63 and living in Whinfell, wished the artist luck but said the encounter with the flying saucer had definitely not been faked.'[8]

The question of whether the Solway Spaceman photograph was an accident or the Coniston UFO picture was faked in many

ways misses the point. In his book on George Adamski, Colin
Bennett sees him as a kind of genius manqué who did not understand the difference between fact, imagination and fantasy. The
problem, suggests Bennett, 'is that in the 20th century we have
lost the relation between Imagination and Fact. For us, with our
"objectivity," Fact and Imagination now longer seed and synthe-
size one another as they did for say the world of the Renaissance....
For us, Imagination has fallen to Entertainment, and Fact emerges
from the screams of billions of tortured laboratory animals.'[9] For
Bennett, anomalous events are a kind of cultural defiance, a desire
to resist the total dominance of rationalism.[10]

It is possible that the UFO phenomenon is far stranger than
we imagine, and that the explanation for it in terms of extrater-
restrial visitors conceals more bizarre realities. Recently, in the
London Review of Books, Nick Richardson reported on the website of the To The Stars Academy, an organisation started by Tom
DeLonge, a member of the band Blink-182, and a long-term UFO
obsessive. Remarking on the wealth of evidence for UFOs on the
site, and the lack of any credible explanation for their existence,
Richardson goes on to suggest that the US government is giving
DeLonge access to this material and allowing him to speculate on
it being of alien origin 'because it's safer to have Tom DeLonge let
us believe in aliens with superior technology that it is to acknowledge that reality itself may be different to what think it is, and that
the US government doesn't understand it either.'[11]

Brantwood

I decided to go to Brantwood, the house in which John Ruskin spent his last years. As I almost always do when I travel to Coniston I took the A591, and turned towards Coniston at Greenodd. The rains came and went, sometimes making it almost impossible to see out of the car windscreen. Making sure that I take the proper turns to get to the east of the lake, where Brantwood is located, was, as always, fraught. This time I shot past the turning, but managed to cross over to the right road at Water Yeat. The road on the east of the lake skirts right next to the water, which is seen through trees and bushes. In summer, in good weather, people treat the lake shore like a beach and set up windbreaks and picnic rugs, though it was not that kind of day.

As it gets nearer to Brantwood, the road diverges from the lakeside and rises up. After a few miles the house itself appears. It is large and has a great position looking right over the lake, but is itself an undistinguished and ramshackle building. It seems strange, ironic even, that one of the great advocates of good architecture should have bought such a mediocre house as Brantwood, but then Ruskin almost certainly wanted it for the view over the lake and to the hills beyond. He bought Brantwood in 1871 for 1,500 pounds, and it became his main residence for the rest of his life, with the garden in particular becoming almost a laboratory for his horticultural ideas. From the windows at the front of the house, looking down on Coniston Water and across to the mountain known as the Old Man of Coniston, the grandeur of the surrounding area is revealed.

Born in 1819, and educated at Oxford, Ruskin is probably best known as possibly the greatest art critic of the nineteenth century, particularly through the five-volume work *Modern Painters*, the first volume of which was published in 1843, and the last two in 1856. *Modern Painters* started as a defence of the work of J. M. W. Turner against his critics, before becoming a far more wide-ranging work. Its advocacy of truth to nature helped inspire the formation of the Pre-Raphaelite brotherhood, a group of young painters, including William Holman Hunt, Dante Gabriel Rossetti and John Everett Millais (who would marry Effie, Ruskin's ex-wife in the mid-1850s). Ruskin was also an important social critic, with books such as *Unto This Last*, and a proto-environmentalist, as evinced in his address 'The Storm-cloud of the Nineteenth Century'. Ruskin also wrote about a great deal of other subjects, including architecture, botany, geology and education, and was involved in many projects to do with the latter in particular. His extraordinary productivity in terms of writing and the wide range of his interests is made manifest in the Cook and Wedderburn edition of his collected works, which runs to thirty-eight thick volumes.

Ruskin wrote prolifically, as the editions of his works prove, and much has been written about him. But in his final decade, words seemed to fail him. In the autumn of 1889 he fell silent, and remained so for several months. Though he did, to some extent, recover, he suffered periods of silence throughout the 1890s, as his mental health deteriorated, periods which increased towards the end of the decade. He died in 1900. (By a strange coincidence in 1889 Friedrich Nietzsche also went mad, and also remained alive until 1900. He too was largely mute in this period. Famously, his madness was supposedly precipitated by the sight of a cabman flogging his horse.)

Ruskin and Nietzsche, two highly articulate men in love with words, the latter originally a professor of philology, are both rendered silent, dumb, which, in the United States in particular, also means stupid. The possession of language is a mark of the human and something that dumb, stupid animals lack. One of the words in French for animal, *bête*, 'beast', also means stupid. Thus, stupidity is explicitly related to animality, and thus to the lack of language. The possession of intelligence, as a specifically human characteristic, is bound up with language use. Animals, who cannot speak, cannot be intelligent. The prevalent attitude was not the case for Ruskin who had a profound reverence for animals, whom he often proclaimed as superior to humans. In *Fors Clavigera* for example, he writes that 'The baboons in Regent's Park—with Mr Darwin's pardon—are of another species; a less passive, and infinitely wittier one.'[1] According to Dinah Birch, Ruskin 'saw no reason for humanity to feel superior over the animal kingdom— even humanity at its most august.'[2] In *The Eagle's Nest: Ten Lectures on the Relation of Natural Science to Art*, Ruskin proclaims that 'All Nature, with one voice—with one glory,—is set to teach you reverence for the life communicated to you from the Father of Spirits. The song of birds, and their plumage; the scent of flowers, their colour, their very existence, are in direct connection with the mystery of that communicated life.'[3] Here, as so often, Ruskin appears extraordinarily prescient. As Birch puts it: 'the issues that he identifies as crucial have continued to be so, and are indeed particularly apparent and often acute in our own very different culture.' She goes on to suggest that this 'is not simply a matter of what Ruskin would have made of Damien Hirst, though that is part of the story. The wider point is that questions surrounding the relations between the animal and the human, between the body and scientific study, and the body and artistic study, lie at the very heart of our millennial culture.'[4]

Part of Ruskin's reverence for animals took the form of a passionate opposition to vivisection and anatomical study. It was this opposition that led to his break with the University of Oxford, despite having been instrumental in founding the Oxford Museum, now known as the University Museum of Natural History. The last straw for Ruskin was the appointment of vivisectionist Sir John Burdon-Sanderson as the first Wayneflete Professor of Physiology in 1882, and the endowment of a new physiology laboratory in

1885. It was in that year Ruskin resigned his professorship, giving his final lecture, pointedly, to an antivivisection group. This not only severed his connection to the university in which he had been involved since an undergraduate and to the art school he had founded, it also, in Birch's words, 'brought his public career as an art teacher and critic to an end'.[5] Thus, even before mental illness literally made him mute or dumb, his sympathy for animals had made him so in metaphorical terms.

At more or less the moment Ruskin (and Nietzsche) fell silent, another Lakeland resident, Beatrix Potter, was giving animals a voice. Of course, speaking animals had been a staple of folk tales and myths almost throughout human history, but Potter is perhaps the first writer whose animal characters, even if they speak and wear clothes, remain at some level real animals. Far from being sentimental anthropomorphic cyphers for human types, her characters are beset with animal affect. That the animals speak emphasises their animality rather than hides it, and in doing so reminds us of our own animal nature. The animal world she depicts is in fact cruel and unsentimental. This was due not just to her deep understanding of the world of animals, but also her powers of visual observation. Among other things, Potter was a gifted amateur scientist with a particular interest in mycology. Her studies of fungi are very striking and indeed beautiful, though far from what people expect from her work. At one point, she tried to present some of her findings to the Linnean Society, but this appeared to have foundered somewhat controversially, perhaps because she was a woman trying to enter a man's world.

Potter lived at High Top Farm in Near Sawrey, only a few miles east of Coniston and Brantwood. The house has been preserved in, or perhaps returned to, the state it was when she was there. Visitors to the house are encouraged to borrow copies of her books to see how she used its rooms and stairwells as the backgrounds of her stories. By the time Potter was publishing her stories, Ruskin was deep in his late madness. Had things been otherwise, he might have appreciated her work as evincing the fidelity to nature he espoused. Ruskin greatly admired the far more sentimental work of Kate Greenaway, not least her portrayal of children. (Fascinatingly, Potter recorded her impression of Ruskin in her diary. She saw him at the Royal Academy in 1884, when she was seventeen and he was sixty-five. She called him 'one of the most ridiculous figures I have seen', and described his old and 'not particularly clean looking' clothes, one of his trouser legs being tucked up in his boot, and his clumsy and failed attempt to put this right.)[6]

Potter can be seen as one of the pioneers of a tradition of modern literature, mostly for children, in which animals are given voices to describe their vicissitudes and sufferings. Rudyard Kipling's *Jungle Book* stories date from around the same time. Among other notable works featuring talking animals are Kenneth Grahame's *The Wind in the Willows*, E. B. White's *Charlotte's Web*, George Orwell's *Animal Farm* and Richard Adams' *Watership Down*. The latter attempts to present rabbits as having a rich and dignified culture and mythology as well as a highly organised society. It also offers a harrowing vision of the kinds of dangers and traumas faced by its lapine protagonists, from disease to human encroachment on their burrows.

In 1977, Adams published his novel *The Plague Dogs*, set in Cumbria, in which the Lakelands farm Lawson Park featured as a government research station devoted to vivisection. Lawson Park is a real place, and was originally owned, and 'emparked', by the Abbey of St Mary in Furness, the ruins of which are still extant in Barrow-in-Furness. In 1537, Lawson Park was sold off as part of the dissolution of the monasteries by Henry VIII, to the Sandys Family. In 1670, Thomas Sandys gave the farms to the parish of Satterthwaite. For over two hundred years it was tenant-farmed, before being purchased in 1897 by John Ruskin's nephew as part of the Brantwood estate, and then in 1910 by Edward John Woodman. From 1920 to 1937 the Hallam family from Liverpool rented it as a holiday home. After being tenant-farmed by a number of others, it was bought in 1947 by the Forestry Commission, and used to house staff. In the 1960s, merchant navy cadets from Liverpool's Riversdale College used it and then from 1970 to 2000, it was a field study centre for sailing, canoeing and climbing for Liverpool Community College.

It is not clear whether Adams was aware that the house in which he placed his fictional research centre once belonged to Ruskin, the passionate opponent of vivisection, a passion evidently shared by Adams. Though not a great book, *Plague Dogs* does bring together some strong themes, including the potentially catastrophic implications of the 'plague' supposedly carried by the dogs, and also a brave attempt to inhabit the interior worlds of the dogs themselves. By making the supposedly idyllic location of a Lakes farmhouse the site of atrocity against animals, Adams does indicate something of the largely unacknowledged uncanniness of the Lake District, the sense that underneath the tourist veneer there lies something far stranger and discomforting, something apocalyptic.

Lawson Park is now the headquarters of Grizedale Arts, the arts organisation that has done much to address the contradictions of our love affair with 'nature', including looking at our relation with our animal others. Working in Cumbria in the late 1990s and early 2000s as artist-in-residence at Grizedale Arts, Marcus Coates made a series of works in which he tried to become an animal. He designed and wore a pair of wooden shoes he named 'stoat stilts', which forced him to walk like a stoat. He also tied himself high up on a tree to become a goshawk. He attached dead birds to his head and ran through Grizedale Forest in an attempt to excite the predatory interest of sparrowhawks.

Coates was commissioned to produce the first image for Grizedale Arts' notorious billboard, which they erected in the middle of Grizedale Forest, much to the disgust of both locals and visitors. Coates' image was a photograph of himself sitting disconsolately in his bedroom in the bed and breakfast he was staying in, wearing antlers and a deer mask, with the bedclothes arranged as a kind of den. It was entitled 'Wild Animal in Its Den'. He also made a number of provocative interventions, including a video of an actor playing a football fan shouting 'who the fuckin' ell are you?' and similar taunts at trees in the forest, the implication being that birdsong is a similar form of aggressive defence of territory.

Discussions of Coates' work often invoke the concept developed by Gilles Deleuze and Felix Guattari of 'becoming animal'. In their book *What Is Philosophy?* Gilles Deleuze and Felix Guattari suggest the 'agony of the rat or the slaughter of a calf remains present in thought not through pity but as the zone of exchange between man and animal in which something of one passes into the other'.[7] One of the ways to think about the sense of apocalypse that pervades our culture is that it reflects the coming end of the human, perhaps literally, in that we may be making the planet unlivable for us at least, but also conceptually. Michel Foucault famously wrote that soon the human, or rather the humanist idea of the human, will disappear like a face drawn in the sand by the sea. Giorgio Agamben demands the stopping or jamming of the anthropogenic machine that produces the division between the human and the animal.[8] One of the principal means by which this machine works is through language, that which distinguishes humans from animals.

One way of doing this may be to stop privileging language as something that makes humans more responsive and aware of the world than animals. In his recent book *Religious Affect*, religious studies scholar Donovan Schaefer is concerned to find alternative explanations for religious and other human behaviour that do not reduce them to linguistic and discursive phenomena. To this end he uses affect theory, in particular the work of Lauren Berlant, Kathleen Stewart, Eve Kosofsky Sedgwick and others. He starts the book with Jane Goodall's description of a group of apes dancing in front of a waterfall, which appears for all intents and purposes to be an expression of religious awe.[9] From this, Schaefer suggests that religion is an artefact of affect and can be found in humans and in non-humans alike, regardless of the possession or otherwise of the capacity for language. Later in the book, Schaefer again invokes the work of Goodall, this time a description of a troupe of chimpanzees' apparently ecstatic celebration after killing an intruder into their territory.[10] He also discusses James Harrod's observations on the death rituals of chimpanzees.[11] This and other evidence of ritual behaviour in relation to outsiders suggests that the 'capacity to draw boundaries between us and them forms somewhere far upstream of the words themselves'.[12]

In an interview with Leyland de la Durantaye, Giorgio Agamben describes walking in the Italian countryside and encountering a horse in a meadow, with whom, through gesture and movement, he claims to have 'communicated perfectly and profoundly' for an hour. For Agamben, this proves that language is not made for communication, but is made for something else, 'something perhaps more important, but also more perilous'. He suggests that 'Language is, in fact, the principle obstacle to communication, which animals know perfectly well. They watch us sometimes, filled by a strange compassion for us, caught up as we are in language. They, too, might have ventured into language, but preferred not to, knowing what might be lost'. He continues that 'I am an animal, even if I belong to a species that lives in unnatural conditions. And it seems to me at times that animals regard me with compassion. I'm touched by this, and feel something akin to shame every time an animal looks at me'.[13]

Brigflatts

The tiny hamlet of Brigflatts is on the way to Sedbergh from where we live. To get to there involves going on the often empty roads that run along the Lune Valley, past Rigmaden Park and turn towards the valley floor past a row of handsome Victorian estate cottages. The road crosses the river over a cast iron bridge, and after a hundred or so yards on the road meets the A683, the main route from the A65 to Sedbergh. The road crosses a tributary of the Lune, the Rawthey, after which Brigflatts is on the right-hand side. It is down a short narrow lane, and consists of a complex of houses, barns, a Quaker Meeting House and a farmhouse at the end.

This reminds me that soon after I started working at Lancaster University, the then vice chancellor made a strategic error when dealing with some student activists. Six students had infiltrated a university-sponsoring 'corporate venturing' event on campus, which featured among other participants, BAE Systems, notorious as arms manufacturers. The students addressed the participants and unfurled a banner. They were in the venue for a few minutes. The university, with considerable misjudgement, had them arrested and prosecuted, decisions that sat ill with the university's liberal, progressive reputation. One of the obvious reasons why this was such a misjudgement on the university's part was that the site in which the event was taking place was (and indeed still is) called The George Fox Building. This led to the students being called the 'George Fox Six'. George Fox was, of course, the founder of the Society of Friends, otherwise known as the Quakers. One of the main elements of Quaker belief is a commitment to pacifism.

I write 'of course' concerning Fox's identity, but until this episode I was more or less unaware of who he was, and not much more informed about the Quakers, who had not impinged much on my life in the south. However, it is hard to avoid encountering Quakerism in the North West, as it is the place where it came into existence. Fox, who was born in 1624 and died in 1691, was extraordinarily peripatetic, travelling all over England preaching his new understanding of Christianity and looking for like-minded souls. The Society of Friends emerged out of Fox's new understanding that the light of Christ was in everyone, a realisation he came to in 1647. In 1652, he felt called by God to Pendle Hill in Lancashire (a place made notorious earlier in the same century for the Pendle witch trials). In his diaries he described the experience.

As we travelled we came near a very great hill, called PENDLE-HILL, and I was moved of the Lord to go up to the top of it; which I did with difficulty, it was so very steep and high. When I was come to the top, I saw the sea bordering upon Lancashire. From the top of this hill the Lord let me see in what places he had a great people to be gathered. As I went down, I found a spring of water in the side of the hill, with which I refreshed myself, having eaten or drunk but little for several days before.[1]

From there he went to Sedbergh to meet with some of the Westmoreland Seekers, a group of non-conformists founded in the early seventeenth century. Fox arrived at Firbank Fell, just outside Sedbergh, where a group of Seekers were gathered at a small chapel.

While others were gone to dinner, I went to a brook, got a little water, and then came and sat down on the top of a rock hard by the chapel. In the afternoon the people gathered about me, with several of their preachers. It was judged there were above a thousand people; to whom I declared God's everlasting truth and Word of life freely and largely for about the space of three hours.[2]

The Seekers present converted to Fox's understanding of Christ being able to speak directly to anyone. This became a major event in the early history of the Society of Friends, and Fox recognised the small hamlet of Brigflatts, near Firbank Fell, as being one of the places that God had caused people to be gathered. In 1675 the second Quaker Meeting House was founded there.

The last time I went to Brigflatts was in late May, in the middle of an extended period of fine weather. The day seemed heavy with summer, and almost unbearably beautiful. It was perhaps the first time I really understood the double meaning of the word sultry, referring to both hot weather, and to a kind of glowering sensuality and sexual attractiveness. It was a Sunday, and, fortuitously, I had arrived at a bit before half past ten, the appointed time of the Friends' weekly meeting. One Friend, an elderly woman with walking sticks, wished me good morning and asked me if I was coming to the meeting. Following the dictum, attributed to a number of mostly musical figures, that you should try everything once, except incest and Morris dancing, I decided to attend.

I knew, roughly, what happened at such meetings. People sat in silence, and every so often one of the attendees would stand up and say something. This is indeed what occurred, but, as is often the case, actual experience is qualitatively different to knowing about something. Apart from anything else, even if no one was speaking, the meeting was far from silent. The worshippers, if that is the word, breathed deeply and noisily, and occasionally seemed to snore. Stomachs rumbled. Bodies shifted noisily on the wooden benches. The Meeting House itself clanked and groaned. Nevertheless, there was a pervasive sense of calm, and also of strangeness. It is uncanny to sit in a room with a handful of other people who are neither trying to interact with each other or distract themselves with books, or phones, or other apparatus. Bar a few water pipes the room appears to be much as it would have been in the late seventeenth century, and sitting there feels like a kind of time travel, especially with the summer light coming through the window as the only illumination. The furnishings have the simplicity more often connected with the Shakers, another seventeenth-century non-conformist sect. In the middle of the room there was a simple wooden table on top of which rested a jug with some wild flowers.

There were only seven people in the room, including myself. About twenty minutes into the meeting a man who had sat at the side of room, looking at pieces of paper, stood and spoke about being an economist before retirement, and used that as a way of thinking about the numbers of Friends in the world. A little later, a woman stood and recited a Quaker hymn and talked about what it means. The elderly woman who had greeted me stood last and started with the observation that life, after all, goes on, and describes two recent funerals of Friends that she has attended, both of which were, according to her, surprisingly joyful. By this point I was getting quite anxious. I had failed to find out how long the meeting and its silence would last. Is it a case, I wondered, of who stands up first? However, almost exactly an hour after it started everyone stood up and shook each other's hand. I was left with the sense of having participated in an event from an entirely different epoch. It is almost as if the light in the room is itself from the seventeenth century. Above all, it was an experience of what it might be like to believe in the immanence of God in the everyday. Sadly, I did not have an epiphany as I sat as still as I could manage in the room.

My reason for visiting Brigflatts was less to do with George Fox, and more to do with the other major figure with which it is connected. The poet Basil Bunting is buried in the Quaker burial ground at Brigflatts, though he never lived there, nor was he a Quaker. He was, however, influenced by both his Quaker schooling at Leighton Park School in the North West of England and also by his teenage visits with his family to Brigflatts. Above all, he was marked for life by his youthful love for Peggy Greenbank, daughter of the local stonemason, whom he first met when she was nine and he fourteen years old. The degree to which this love remained with him is hard to overstate despite his having ended their relationship in 1918 by failing to answer a letter. Bunting led a fairly extraordinary life, including a spell in prison as a Quaker-influenced conscientious objector during the First World War (he refused even the option of working on the land, on the grounds that it would free a farm labourer to fight); a peripatetic existence in the interwar period in England, Europe and the United States, including periods in Rapallo as a protégé of Ezra Pound.

His dedication to poetry led him to write some of the masterpieces of poetic Modernism, including 'Villon', 'Chomei at Toyama' and 'The Well at Lycopolis' in that period. The same dedication and his refusal to countenance a real job also led to the breakdown of his marriage to Marion Gray Culver in 1936. She fled back to her native United States, taking both their daughters with her, and while pregnant with a son that Bunting never met. The trauma of this desertion led to him more or less ceasing to write poetry for several decades, with the exception of a few of his odes, his longish poem 'The Spoils' and one or two other works. In the Second World War, despite having been a conscientious objector in the First World War, he volunteered for the RAF, and then, having learnt classical Persian to translate the poet Ferdowsi, he worked for British Intelligence in Tehran. He stayed there after the War, working for the British Embassy, until expelled by Mossadegh in 1952. After this, having been forgotten as a great Modernist pioneer, he worked in Newcastle for the *Evening Chronicle*. It was in Newcastle in the 1960s that a younger generation of poets rediscovered his work and set about restoring his reputation. This renewed interest clearly revived his poetic gifts, and he wrote what many regard as one of the greatest works of poetry of the twentieth century, *Briggflatts* (Bunting added the extra 'g'), which returns to the point at which he started, in and around the Quaker Meeting House in the Lune Valley. It begins:

Brag, sweet tenor bull,
descant on Rawthey's madrigal,
each pebble its part

for the fells' late spring.
Dance tiptoe, bull,
black against may.
Ridiculous and lovely
chase hurdling shadows
morning into noon.
May on the bull's hide
and through the dale
furrows fill with may...[3]

Briggflatts celebrates, above all, Bunting's great lost love, Peggy Greenbank. After the poem's publication it seems that Greenbank and he not only met, but rekindled their relationship. Bunting's biographer is reticent about this episode, but there is a sense, not least from Peggy Greenbank's account, that Bunting was interested in the memory of his lost love, as she was in the beginning, rather than in a woman in her sixties.

The poem thus becomes an allegory of our relation to the divine and to language. Members of the Society of Friends believe they can directly experience God in the everyday. This is, as with almost all religion, an attempt to recover a lost plenitude or Edenic state. As Hilary Hinds puts it, 'the Quaker dissolution of the carnal self seemed genuinely to allow for that access of "divine pleni-tude" in the indwelling Christ, who could remake the believing subject, erase the fallen self and institute a state of prelapsarian perfection in that subject – a condition that was both fully human (as were Adam and Eve before the fall) but also perfected in their relation with the divine.'[4]

For the spiritually inclined but atheist Bunting, such a pleni-tude was perhaps to be found in the resurrection of lost love and of the lost Eden of Brigflatts. But, like Orpheus, Bunting cannot look directly at his love without losing her, and thus must keep her still as only a memory. In the end there is only the poem, only lan-guage. One can see this, perhaps, as Giorgio Agamben does; with the 'death of God' we come face to face with language itself. 'God is the name of the preexistence of language,' which means that 'human beings are thrown into language without having a voice or a divine word to guarantee them a possibility of escape from the infinite play of meaningful propositions. Thus we finally find ourselves alone with our words; for the first time we are truly alone with language, abandoned without any final foundation.'[5]

Dentdale

One morning I performed an aleatory practice that I indulge in quite a lot, a digital throw of the dice, in which I put two or more words or phrases into Google and see what comes up (otherwise known as 'google-whacking'). I put the name of Charles Fort, the great researcher of abnormal occurrences, along with 'Cumberland'. Fort is a particularly apt subject for this process as he was fascinated by random events such as the phenomenon of rocks that apparently fall from the sky, sometimes known as 'thunderstones'. This randomness seems an appropriate metaphor for what falls out of the Web. Fort famously spent most of his time in libraries reading decades' worth of scientific journals and newspapers looking for accounts of anomalous events that could not be explained easily by scientific orthodoxy. He enjoyed mocking the anxious rhetoric by which scientists tried to distance themselves from the inexplicability of what had happened. Among his main sources of both evidence and rhetorical unease was George James Symons' *Monthly Meteorological Magazine*, founded in 1866. Symons was the founder of the British Rainfall Organisation as well as editor of the magazine. In his research Fort finds an account of a stone falling from the sky in what was then Westmorland, now Cumbria, just over the other side of the Lune River from Kirkby Lonsdale.

Then comes the instance of a man, his wife, and his three daughters, at Casterton, Westmoreland, who were looking out at their lawn, during a thunderstorm, when they 'considered,' as Mr. Symons expresses it, that they saw a stone fall from the sky, kill a sheep, and bury itself in the ground.

They dug.

They found a stone ball.[1]

Clearly, Fort sees Symons' use of the word 'considered' as evincing a kind of pre-emptive scepticism. Fort goes on to describe, presumably from Symons' account, how the object was exhibited at a meeting of the Royal Meteorological Society by one Mr. C. Carus-Wilson, and how it was described in the Journal's list of exhibits as a 'sandstone' ball, and by Symons as 'sandstone'.[2]

Fort points out that finding a piece of sandstone in the ground is not surprising but what was actually discovered in Casterton was something far rarer and more complex, 'a ball of hard, ferruginous quartzite, about the size of a cocoanut, weight about twelve pounds... there is a suggestion not only of symmetry but of structure in this object'.[3] Fort also notes 'an amusing little touch in the indefinite allusion to "a man," who with his un-named family, had "considered" that he had seen a stone fall'. The man was, in fact, 'the Rev. W. Carus-Wilson, who was well-known in his day'.[4]

William Carus-Wilson was indeed 'well-known' in his day, though possibly not for reasons he would have liked. He perhaps would have preferred to be known for founding and editing the magazines *The Friendly Visitor* and *The Children's Friend*, or for starting a school for the daughters of clergymen at Cowan Bridge in Yorkshire. In fact, he is known for the latter but not in a good way. One of the pupils at the school was Charlotte Brontë, who was there, with her sisters Maria, Elizabeth and, briefly, Emily, in the 1820s. Cowan Bridge School is the model for Lowood School in Charlotte's novel *Jane Eyre*, to which Jane is sent, and which she hates. Brontë based the character of Robert Brocklehurst on Carus-Wilson, and the resemblance was close enough for him to consider suing her for defamation.

In another episode of google-whacking, I put in the words 'Derrida' and 'Bunting', just to see if anyone had brought together the great French philosopher with my favourite modernist poet, Basil Bunting (who also has strong connections with the North West). I did not find much but came across an entry for a blog called 'Writing the Messianic', with an epigraph from Derrida, and then this short text.

Basil Bunting and Jonathan Williams
Bunting to Jonathan Williams
whether it is a stone
next to a stone or
a word next to a word
it is the glory[5]

Immediately intrigued, I googled 'Jonathan Williams' and found out that he was an American poet, involved with Black Mountain College, founder of the Jargon Society, a small press devoted to idiosyncratic productions involving poetry and art, collector of outsider art and an accumulator of found knowledge and folkways. I also discovered that in his later life he and Tom Meyer, his partner, had lived part of the time in Dentdale, in a house named Corn Close, about eleven or so miles from where I live, close enough for me to cycle there, and take a look at the house and wonder about the anomalous presence of two gay American poets in the remote countryside of Dentdale.

Williams was an extremely interesting character. As well as being a respected poet, he was also a publisher, a photographer and a collector of unusual art, as well as bon viveur. He dropped out of Princeton after a year in the 1940s, studied etching, engraving and printmaking in New York and typography, etching and photography at the Illinois Institute of Technology. Finally, he found himself at Black Mountain College, where he studied under Charles Olson, at the same time as the summer visits of John Cage and Robert Rauschenberg. He founded the Jargon Society, which, despite its name, was a small press, with David Ruff in 1951. Its first publication *GARBAGE LITTERS THE IRON FACE OF THE SUN'S CHILD* was a single sheet of yellow paper, more of a handbill than a book, with its title and the words JARGON 1, along with a woodcut by David Ruff on the obverse, and the poem itself on the other. It was handset in Lydian type, a calligraphic sans serif designed by Warren Chappell for American Type Founders in 1938. Only fifty copies were produced, marking the 'beginning of one of the greatest of the great postwar American private presses.'[6] The Jargon Society published 116 books, each numbered and each different. The list includes works by Charles Olson, Robert Creeley, Lorine Neidecker, Kenneth Patchen, Ronald Johnson, as well as volumes on the *The Work of Joe Webb: Appalachian Master of Rustic Architecture*, and *White Trash Cooking*. Each Jargon Society publication looks entirely different.

The story of how Williams and his partner Thomas Meyer found themselves in Dentdale is curious. It is recounted in *Corn Close: A Cottage in Dentdale*, which is also the most recent, or perhaps the last, of the Jargon Society publications, number 116, with essays by Meyer and Anne Midgette, and photographs by Reuben Cox. Apparently Williams' biography on the back cover of *An Ear in Bartram's Tree*, his selected poems, published in 1969, claimed that he lived in North Carolina (true), and in a 'seventeenth-century stone cottage in Upper Wharfedale, Yorkshire, England', which was not true. However, his patron, the oilman and painter, Donald B. Anderson, who supported both Williams and the Jargon Society, proposed to make it true. He offered Williams and Meyer the use of a house in England if they found it and did it up. At the suggestion of Basil Bunting they looked in Dentdale and found Corn Close. For thirty years, from 1969 to 1999, Williams and Meyer spent part of the year there, entertaining an extraordinary array of visitors.

The book by Williams that most directly engages with the North West is his collaboration with the artist Tom Phillips, entitled *Imaginary Postcards (Clints Grikes Grips Glints)*, published in 1975 by Trigram Press. (In fact, 150 copies were printed and distributed by the press to various friends, before a dispute about the design between Trigram and one of the authors led to the book never being officially published.) The form the book takes is of images on the left-hand page and poems on the right, with, at best, an oblique relation between the two. The poems are brief, comic and sometimes scatological and often not more than a witty observation. One of the briefest, and perhaps my favourite, is as follows:

A Sign in the Lune Valley Reveals
The Way of the Triffids
HEAVY
PLANT
CROSSING[7]

The poem by Williams that I found on the Web suggests a familiarity with one of the most striking sights in Dentdale and all over the north of England. Drystone walls may be one of the great architectural and sculptural achievements in this country. Tens of thousands of miles of such walls are found in Britain, traversing across some of the most inhospitable terrain. They are all over Cumbria, Lancashire and North Yorkshire. When we first arrived in the North, these walls were one of the features of the landscape we quickly noticed, not least for how they demark the landscape and give it a particular austere and robust feel.

In this respect, Jonathan Williams' work seems exceptionally relevant. He took the idea of found language to extremes. As Robert Morgan suggests, in *The Nation*, Williams uses, more than any other poet, 'the Objectivist principle, the idea that a poem is first of all a linguistic, phonetic, graphic object. He takes the language eroding right now in our mouths and cultivates it, shapes it, and speaks it to life.'[8]

I discover later that the line after 'The Glory of it' in the poem found on the internet, written by Jonathan Williams for Basil Bunting, is 'The craft of it', and later he writes of 'solid, common, vulgar words/the ones you can touch/the ones that yield/and a respect for the music...'[9]

In his book *Reflections on the Lakes*, John Wyatt writes about the building of a dry wall, which he describes as 'a fascinating work of art', and a 'heavy three-dimensional jigsaw puzzle... locking it together us a therapeutic exercise'. Once the line of the wall is decided, 'the soil is dug to about six inches, or less if the ground is firm'. A drystone wall is 'really two walls', with lines of stones laid on either side, filled in with smaller stone fragments, known as 'heartings'.[10] At certain levels large stones, known as 'through', go through both sides and lock them together. The walls narrow towards the top, and 'are finished with "cams", stones laid on their edges and all leaning in one direction'.[11] Sometimes alternate tall and short cams are used to make a castellated effect. Wyatt describes how much he admires the craft of making something so apparently simple, and describes the perfection of a wall he knows in the Duddon valley. It is 'so perfectly made that I have to stop and enjoy the sight of it. What a man was this that could create such a thing of beauty from crude untooled rock? The stones are set absolutely flush, the line and the tapering perfect. I get more enjoyment out of seeing that wall than I would get from seeing a great master's work in an art gallery'.[12]

Wyatt describes watching his driver, George, make a wall.

He always pleaded he was no expert, but, like all craftsmen, he made it look so simple. Having picked up a stone he would never put it down, he would find a place where it fit somewhere. And, like all the best wallers I have watched, he would not place the stone in position, but offer it towards its place and drop it there, or throw it. The solidity of the 'clunk' as it landed told him that it fitted and should stay there. If it was not quite right the sound would be different and the stone would rock, in which case he would pick it up and turn it round or drop it in somewhere else.[13]

This notion of the musicality of stones reminds me that in the museum in Keswick in the north Lake District there are a number of 'lithophones', or 'rock harmonicas'. One, dating back to 1785, 'consists of 16 stones embracing two diatonic octaves plus one note'.[14] These stones were found by a local publisher of maps, Peter Crosthwaite. Eight were discovered on the bed of the river Greta and eight on nearby Skiddaw peak. Some decades later another native of Keswick, Joseph Richardson, produced a larger lithophone, with an eight-octave range. By the time he had finished building his instrument in 1840 it had reduced his family to poverty, but he was able to recover financially by firstly touring the North of England, then playing in London, including a performance at Buckingham Palace in 1848, in front of Queen Victoria and Prince Albert. He and his family went on to tour all over Europe and nearly made it to the United States, though this fell through because of the illness of Robert, the youngest and most talented of the family band, who subsequently died. There were other 'rock' bands from Keswick, such as that of Daniel Till and his sons, who did tour America and whose Musical Stones are now in the Metropolitan Museum in New York.

In the early 2000s, Keswick Museum was approached by Grizedale Arts and asked if they would collaborate with New York musician and artist Brian Dewan. With the help of Jamie Barnes, the duty officer at Keswick Museum, Dewan composed an hour-long suite of seven 'movements' for the Stones. This was performed on a special frame and sound box using thirty-one of the sixty-one stones, on the shores of Coniston Water, across from Brantwood, John Ruskin's house, as part of the Coniston Water Festival in 2005, which had been revived by Grizedale Arts. The performance, which was amplified, could be heard across the lake and in Coniston, and also on a specially set up short-wave radio station. One of the results of this revival of the Stones was to be featured in a BBC documentary presented by Evelyn Glennie, entitled, predictably perhaps, 'The World's First Rock Band', and which also featured one of the oldest lithophones from a museum in Paris.

That the performance was directed towards Brantwood was not an arbitrary decision. Ruskin was fascinated by rocks and stones and was a keen amateur geologist, among other things, and was so impressed by Richardson's Musical Stones, remarking that they had given him 'a new musical pleasure', that, in 1884, he commissioned a set to be made for him by William Till, Daniel Till's son. However, other sounds made by tapping rocks were far less welcome for Ruskin. 'If only the geologists would leave me alone, I could do very well, but those dreadful hammers! I hear the clink of them at the end of every cadence of the Bible verses.'[15]

Coniston

Coniston is at the north-west edge of Coniston Water. St Andrews Church is more or less in the middle of the village. It's not a particularly exciting church but is notable for the occupants of its graveyard. Ruskin is there, commemorated by the extraordinary cross designed by G. M. Collingwood, who is also buried there, with his wife, in a plot next to Ruskin's. Their son, the historian, philosopher and archaeologist, R. G. Collingwood, is interred alongside. James Hewitson, a recipient of the Victoria Cross in the First World War, born in Coniston, is there. A more recent grave, in the overflow graveyard, contains the body of someone whose only connection with Coniston is to have died, in dramatic circumstances, on the lake itself. In 1967, Donald Campbell flipped his K7 Bluebird boat while returning to his starting point to make a second attempt to break the world water speed record. He had decided not to wait until the wash from the first attempt of the day had subsided. Having achieved a top speed of 328 mph, the boat started to bounce, then decelerate, and finally executed a somersault, and then sank. Campbell's final words were recorded, and offer a macabre example of the almost impossible testimony of someone in the act of dying.

Full nose up... Pitching a bit down here... coming through our own wash... er getting straightened up now on track... rather closer to Peel Island... and we're tramping like mad... and er... FULL POWER... er tramping like hell OVER. I can't see much and the water's very bad indeed... I'm galloping over (I can't get over) the top... and she's (actually) giving a hell of a bloody row in here... I can't see anything... I've got the bows out... I'm going... U-hh...

At the time neither the boat nor Campbell's body was recovered. Only his helmet and Mr Whoppit, his teddy bear, were found, floating on the surface. (Mr Whoppit can now be seen in a glass case attached to Campbell's gravestone in Coniston.) It was not until 2001 that his body was recovered, along with the remains of Bluebird. At his widow's request he was buried in Coniston. The ceremony took place on 12 September 2001, and was thus somewhat overshadowed by the events in New York on the previous day. His sister had objected to his burial, and to the raising of the boat, preferring that both remained where they had sunk in good nautical tradition.

This made me think of the lake as a 'space of death', a phrase employed by Sarah Cormack in her book on the rituals and practices of burial in Roman Asia Minor, which she relates to Michel Foucault's concept of 'heterotopia'.[1] Foucault's aim was to explore a more complex conception of space than allowed for in scientific modernity. Following Gaston Bachelard, he suggests that 'we do not live in a homogeneous and empty space, but on the contrary in a space thoroughly imbued with quantities and perhaps thoroughly fantasmatic as well'.[2] Foucault claims that he is particularly interested in sites that 'have the curious property of being in relation to all the other sites, but in such a way as to suspect, neutralize, or invert the set of relations they happen to designate, mirror, or reflect'.[3] Foucault distinguishes between 'utopias', which, by definition, have no real place, and 'heterotopias', which do exist, are found in all cultures and are formed in the very institution of society.[4] They simultaneously represent, contest and invert the other, real sites in society. Examples he gives include those found in 'so-called primitive societies', which are usually 'privileged or sacred or forbidden places that are reserved for the individual who finds himself in a state of crisis with respect to the society or the environment in which he lives: adolescents, women during the menstrual period or in labour, the old, etc.'[5] In our society heterotopias of crisis are being supplanted by heterotopias of deviance, such as rest homes, prisons and psychiatric clinics.[6]

With Campbell's death, Coniston Water becomes, or perhaps reveals itself as, a kind of heterotopia. The captain of the steam gondola run by the National Trust, which takes passengers along and across Coniston Water, still points out where Campbell sunk, and there remains a sense of the lake as a space for the dead. Ruskin described Coniston as the 'Unter-Walden of England', Unter-Walden being a Swiss canton he particularly loved, and which, in his great early work *Modern Painters*, he writes, in Hilton's words, 'with strange intimations of death and celebrates quiet lives pursued and completed in lakeside valleys beneath precipices and forests of vine'.[7] Brantwood itself was 'a dark house overshadowed by trees'. He also connected it and the valley in which it sits with a kind of easeful death. When suffering a near-fatal illness in Matlock in 1871, he felt a longing 'to lie down in Coniston Water'.[8] From his study in Brantwood, Ruskin would be looking at the very spot where, in 1967, nearly a hundred years later, Campbell flipped his boat.

His presence, or rather the presence of his corpse, on the lake bed re-articulates our relation to the lake itself. No longer just a surface to be used at our leisure, it is revealed as a depth, and thus as a different kind of space, inimical to our life, pocketed, or perhaps invaginated, in the landscape. It is a 'space of death' that exists in the midst of our space of life, but heterogeneous to it. The lake's surface is a mirror not just in the sense of reflecting the world around but inverting it. Though Campbell's body is now in the graveyard, the sense of his presence or perhaps absence on the lake bed remains strong. As I write, the Bluebird K7 is still being restored by a team of volunteers. The plan is to return it to Coniston Water for a run (though at no more than 100 mph), before it is given to the Ruskin Museum in the village. The space in which it will be housed has already been built, and remains more or less empty, another strange absence. The presence of the Bluebird is expected to bring a considerable number of extra visitors to the village, drawn as much by the legend of Campbell's tragic death as by his achievements.

The Campbell death cult that Coniston intends to exploit does reveal something more general about the Lake District, that the actual lakes, waters, meres, are all implicitly or explicitly heterotopic. They are spaces within the space of the Lake District as a place of the living that are inimical to human life. This is perhaps most explicit in the case of those artificial lakes created as reservoirs such as Haweswater. In 1929, Parliament passed an act making it possible for Manchester Corporation to flood the beautiful Mardale Valley in order to supply water for the city. This necessitated the abandonment of two villages, Mardale Green and Measand. Sometimes, when the water levels drop, it is said that the remains of Mardale Green can be seen. At the same time the lakes are a location of heterotopic playfulness, especially involving boats and other watercraft. Foucault describes the ship as follows: 'it is a floating part of space, a placeless place, that lives by itself, closed in on itself and at the same time poised in the infinite ocean.'⁹ Coniston is one of the inspirations for the unnamed lake in Arthur Ransome's *Swallows and Amazons* series of books, in which children exploit the possibilities of the lake as a kind of heterotopic space away from the strictures and norms of their everyday life.

Campbell named all his cars and boats Bluebird. His father had done more or less the same, though he called his vehicles Blue Bird. The younger Campbell truncated the two words to distinguish his vehicles from his father's. Sir Malcolm Campbell had been originally inspired to use this name by Maurice Maeterlink's opera *The Blue Bird of Happiness*, about two children seeking happiness. As the website for the Ruskin Museum in Coniston puts it: 'The pursuit of happiness, so close, yet tantalisingly beyond reach, seemed to symbolise his own determined pursuit of ever faster speeds.'

Perhaps this explains his repetitive pursuit of these speed records. In 'Beyond the Pleasure Principle', Sigmund Freud asserts that 'we may venture to make the assumption that there really exists in psychic life a repetition-compulsion, which goes beyond the pleasure-principle'. He suggests that there is an instinct, an urge inherent in organic life to restore an earlier state of things which the living entity has been obliged to abandon under the pressure of external disturbing forces.[10]

Thus for Freud, 'The goal of all life is death', and even that 'The inanimate was there before the animate'. This connects to Freud's anxious engagement with what he called 'the oceanic feeling', described to him in a letter from Romain Rolland, and which he adverts to in *Civilization and Its Discontents*; 'It is a feeling which he would like to call a sensation of "eternity"',... One may, he thinks, rightly call oneself religious on the ground of this oceanic feeling alone, even if one rejects ever belief and every illusion'.[11]

In the letter, Rolland questioned Freud on an aspect of religion he felt the latter had not considered; 'the simple and direct fact of the feeling of the 'eternal' (which, can very well not be eternal, but simply without perceptible limits, and like oceanic, as it were)'. In *Civilization and Its Discontents*, Freud, who had never experienced this oceanic feeling, wrote that he could 'imagine that the oceanic feeling could become connected with religion later on. That feeling of oneness with the universe which is its ideational content sounds very like a first attempt at the consolations of religion, like another way taken by the ego of denying the dangers it sees threatening it in the external world'.[12]

Klaus Theleweit suggests that 'Freud strives to go upward; for him that whole oceanic business is somehow under water, dark and threatening. With his seemingly harmless remark about "oceanic feeling" Rolland appears to have struck a nerve; he has provoked a side of Freud that is openly afraid of the possibility of limitlessness in humans'.[13] For Freud, the oceanic feeling is bound up with a desire to return to the womb as a state of paradise, and to merge with the mother. In this context, it is interesting to note that Campbell was both an inveterate womaniser and a devotee of spiritualism. Campbell often consulted the medium Marjorie

Staves, including right up to the crash in which he was killed. His widow Tonia claimed that after his death he 'refused to leave her alone', with his spirit often visiting her. Tonia was also candid about his love of women, proclaiming that 'Donald was a very naughty boy'.[14]

Coniston is where the murder victim known as the 'Lady in the Lake' was found. In 1976, primary school teacher Carol Park, from Leece, near Barrow, went missing. She had apparently been depressed. Her husband, Gordon Park, also a teacher, claimed that he did not report her disappearance as she had been absent for periods at other times, and had always returned. It was only when she failed to come back in time for the new term that people became suspicious, though at the time her body was not found. In 1997, amateur divers discovered her body on a ledge seventy-foot deep in Lake Coniston. Had the body not settled on the ledge, and had gone to the lake bottom, it would probably have never been found. The corpse had been put in a pinafore dress, arranged in a foetal position, wrapped in a series of plastic and canvas bags, bound with ropes and weighed down with rocks and lead piping. She appeared to have been killed through blunt trauma, possibly with an ice axe. Gordon Park was arrested, though the first trial collapsed; in 2004 he was retried after a prisoner who claimed to have shared his cell while he awaited trial came forward to say that Park had confessed to murdering his wife, because she was having an affair. Park was convicted, sentenced to life imprisonment and told he must serve at least fifteen years. He hanged himself after an appeal against his conviction failed. The case and conviction remain controversial, with Park's children still seeking to exonerate him.

Park is not the only Lakeland 'Lady in the Lake'. In 1976, Peter Hogg murdered his wife Margaret, and dumped her body in Wastwater. The body was found eight years later during the search for a missing French backpacker, Veronique Marr. (Wastwater, England's deepest lake, at eighty metres, is also known for its underwater gnome garden forty-eight metres down. Intended as a secret attraction for divers, it has led to several fatalities, and has been removed, though it is rumoured that it has been reinstated at a depth below that which police divers are allowed to go.) Sheena Owlitt's dead body was dumped by her husband in Crummock Water in 1988, and found three weeks later. That all the husbands in these cases were convicted suggests that this form of body disposal is not very sensible, though of course there may be many more undiscovered ladies and possibly even gentlemen lying at the bottom of various lakes.

The Lady in the Lake, the 1946 film that gave these cases their tabloid name, is a curiosity inasmuch as it is entirely shot from the point of view of the detective protagonist. This in turn makes it an apt name for the murder case, which seems based on a paranoia about female behaviour. For Slavoj Žižek, this aspect of the film produces 'an undeniable sense of dissatisfaction, an impression of failure; they produce a feeling of claustrophobic closure, as if we found ourselves imprisoned in a psychotic universe without symbolic openness'.[15] He suggests that 'we long continually for release from the "glasshouse" of the detective's gaze, so that we can take a "free" and objective view of the action'. Above all, by 'prohibiting the objective shot' the film 'produces an effect of paranoia'. Without the object point of view, 'what is seen is continually menaced by the unseen, and the very proximity of objects to the field of view becomes threatening'. In particular, '[W]hen a woman approaches the camera, for instance, we experience her presence as an aggressive intervention into the sphere of our intimacy'.[16]

This gives a sense of the anxiety felt by men about the threat of what Andrea Freud Loewenstein calls 'engulfing women'.[17] The term 'engulfing' originally referred to seas and whirlpools, and Loewenstein's phrase is a reminder of the relation between water and the feminine, which is both allure and threat. In his book *Male Fantasies*, Klaus Theleweit traces the relation between tropes of flooding and women: 'Over and over again: the women-in-the-water; woman as water, as a stormy, cavorting, cooling ocean, a raging stream, a waterfall; as a limitless body of water that ships pass through, with tributaries, pools, surfs, and deltas; woman as the enticing (or perilous) deep'.[18]

Elterwater

The A591 north from Windermere passes the entrances to many of the houses built by the rich industrialists of Victorian and Edwardian times, most of which are now hotels. Driving along it remains a fairly domesticated experience, with the lake itself mostly hidden from view for the car passenger. Only when approaching Low Wood, about two and a half miles from Windermere, are the lake itself and the mountains on the other side visible, and it is possible to get a sense of the drama of the Lake District. Occasionally, when a heavy mist sits on the lake, the road seems to pass an absolute void, as if nothing existed beyond its western edge. On other days though, this drive can be a sublime experience, especially when the light is on the far mountains. After Low Wood, the road bends round the lake and enters Water Head, the bay at the top of Windermere at which the ferries dock. From here it is possible to go either into Ambleside, or to bypass it and go over the narrow little bridge that crosses the river Rothay, and drive into the heart of the Lakes. At this point, the scenery becomes far more intense, with the hills rising on either side of narrow valleys and the roads following the outer contours of those valleys.

The A593 takes one through Clappergate and then to Skelwith Bridge, at which point a right turn goes to Elterwater along the valley in which the Rathay river runs. The road sits slightly above the valley floor and angulates round until it hits the broader point at which Elterwater itself is to be found. If you drive past the main village, you come to the Langdale Hotel and Spa, a complex of hotel buildings, lodges, cottages and barns, built on what they describe in their publicity as a 'gentleman's residence'. Opposite is the site of what was the Elterwater Gunpowder Works since 1824 until the end of the Second World War. It seems, initially at least, to be a strange place to site such a works, though the explanation is straightforward: gunpowder was an important element in mining and quarrying, two major local industries, and a key component of gunpowder, along with saltpetre and sulphur, was charcoal. Sites such as Elterwater offered access to both wood and water, the latter needed to power the manufacturing process. Until the emergence of dynamite and gelignite, Cumbria was the main source of explosive materials in Britain. However, by the 1930s the fall in demand led to the closure of all the Cumbrian gunpowder works.

In 1944 the site, known as Cylinders after the storage cylinders used by the works, was purchased by landscape architect Harry Pierce, in order to develop it into a garden, arboretum and small-holding. Pierce had worked for the great garden designer Thomas Mawson. In 1946, he saw a portrait of local Ruskin expert Dr George Ainslie Johnson in an Ambleside shop window and decided to commission the artist to paint his portrait. The painter turned out to be that most unlikely of Lakeland residents, the Dada artist and poet Kurt Schwitters, who had recently moved to Cumbria with his partner Edith Thomas and was trying to make a living there as an artist. It was in the grounds of Cylinders that Schwitters made his last 'Merzbau', the Merzbarn, and thus made the Lake District the location of one of the last major works by a member of the early twentieth-century European avant-garde. The Merzbauten were extraordinary constructions made in various interiors composed of three-dimensional, sculptural accretions and additions to the spaces in question.

That Ruskin, the great proclaimer of art's higher purpose, should somehow connect to the arch-Dadaist Schwitters is not as strange as it might seem. In her essay on Schwitters in England, Sarah Wilson suggests that it was Ruskin 'who precipitated, with the famous Ruskin-Whistler trial, the originary point of departure for modernism, not merely in Anglo-american terms. ("The dadaists belonged to a world which, still, remembered and read John Ruskin" wrote Stefan Themerson, explicating Schwitters.)'[1]

How Schwitters ended up in the Lake District is bound up
with the tragic history of war and displacement that characterised
the first half of the twentieth century. Born in Hanover in 1887,
Schwitters was trained as an artist and originally worked as a post-
impressionist, though his experiences in the First World War both
made his work darker and also showed him the possibilities of a
kind of machine aesthetic. After the War and some initial success
he became involved with the Berlin Dada, and by the early 1920s
was producing the work for which he became famous, the collages,
the Merzbauten and the poetical and sound works.

In 1937, he fled Germany and found his way to Norway, where
he started the construction of another Merzbau in the garden of
his house near Oslo. In 1940, he left Norway, after the Nazi invasion, for the United Kingdom, where he was interned on the Isle
of Man. After being released he lived in London until the end
of the War. It was while in London that he met the woman who
would be his partner until his death, Edith Thomas, known by him
as 'Wantee' because she was always offering to make cups of tea.
It was also in London during the War that he found out that his
Hanover Merzbau had been destroyed in the bombing and that his
wife Helga had died of cancer. In 1945, Wantee and he moved to
the Lake District, having first visited in 1942. Having encountered
Harry Pierce, Schwitters was able to devote time to making the
Merzbarn at Cylinders.

The entrance to Cylinders is a green wooden gate set back
from the road, with the drystone wall folded in towards it. On the
wall, a slate plaque bears the words 'Kurt Schwitters Merzbarn'.
Passing through the gate leads to a slightly curved rough path at
the end of which there is a low building, which turns out not to be
the Merzbarn itself. Though made of stone rather than wood, it has
something of the air of a Russian dacha, as seen in Tarkovsky's film
Mirror, or a Swedish *hytt*, a building intended as a summer retreat.
Its bohemian quality is enhanced by the presence of a plastic yurt
to the left of the path. The Merzbarn is to the right, and turns out to

be more like a small stone shed than a barn. It has an open space at the further end, on the left of which there is a door leading to a bare room, at the other end of which there is a full-scale colour photograph of Schwitters' construction. The original was moved in the mid-1960s to the Hatton Gallery in Newcastle, where it can still be seen.

Almost all of Schwitters' artistic activities can be seen as different forms of collage, from the famous collages themselves, through his experiments in language and poetry, to his Merzbauten. Collage, described by Gregory Ulmer as 'the single most revolutionary formal innovation to occur in our century', is an explosive artistic strategy, in which the supposed coherence of the totality of our world is blown apart by the juxtaposition of elements ripped out of their original context.[2] It is an appropriate form for a century in which the fissile possibilities of the atom will be exploited to produce extraordinary amounts of potentially destructive energy. It is also prescient in relation to the world of sampling, mashing up and mixing, which characterises our digital culture. It is perhaps therefore fitting that Schwitters tried to build his last Merzbau, the Merzbarn in a disused gunpowder factory. Here is Schwitters' own instructions for making a Merz work of art.

Make nets fire wave and run off into lines, thicken into surfaces. Net the nets. Make veils blow, soft folds fall, make cotton drip and water gush. Curl up air, soft and white, through thousand candle power arc lamps. Then take wheels and axles, hurl them up and make them sing. Mighty erections of aquatic giants. Axles dance mid-wheel, roll globes barrel, cogs flare, teeth find a sewing machine that yawns. Turning upward or bowed down, the sewing machine beheads itself, feet up. Take a dentist drill or meat grinder or car track scraper. Take buses and pleasure cars, bicycles, tandems and their tires. Take lights and deform them as brutally as you can, make locomotives crash into one another. Explode steam boilers to make railroad mystic, petticoats, shoes, and false hair. For all I care take man traps, automatic pistols, the tin fish in the funnel. Take in short everything from the hair net of the high class lady to the propellor of the S.S. Leviathan, always bearing in mind the dimensions required by the work. Now begin to wedge your materials to one another.[3]

This seems to anticipate what French philosopher Jean-Luc Nancy calls 'struction', which goes beyond both construction, deconstruction and reconstruction. Nancy derives 'struction' from *struo*, to amass or to heap. It is this sense of the heap, the 'non-assembled assembly' that is no longer 'a question of order or organization that is implied by con- and in-struction'.[4] As Nancy describes it:

we are in a spiraling, growing pile of pieces, parts, zones, fragments, slivers, particles, elements, outlines, seeds, kernels, clusters, points, meters, knots, arborescences, projections, proliferations, and dispersions according to which we are now more than ever taken hold of, interwoven into, absorbed into, and dislodged from a prodigious mass that is unstable, moving, plastic, and metamorphic, a mass that renders the distinction between 'subject' and 'object' or between 'man' and 'nature' or 'world' less and less possible for us.[5]

This sounds like a description of the Merzbau in Hanover, in which, as Marjorie Perloff puts it, 'the piles of freestanding "rubbish" that constitute Schwitters' architectural assemblage were in constant flux as the added or subtracted items and created new configurations with the use of wood, cardboard, iron scraps, broken furniture, print media, railway tickets, playing cards, and so on'.[6]

Schwitters' building of the Merzbarn in the context of the Lake District is itself a kind of collage, a juxtaposition of a European avant-garde modernist artwork in the very heart of English Romanticism. Schwitters' own presence there appears as a kind of strange collision, one that barely made sense. When Mary Birkett, founder of Abbott Hall in Kendal, discovered that Schwitters had lived and died in Ambleside, she asked around in the town about him, but nobody had heard of a famous avant-garde artist living there. Eventually, somebody did admit to remembering a gentle madman who painted portraits for a few pounds.

Schwitters is one of those rare artists who produced equally interesting work in both visual and verbal form. Others include David Jones and William Blake. Yet, perhaps because of academic specialisation, such figures are rarely appreciated for the full range of their abilities. In Schwitters' case, this has meant the comparative neglect of his literary work. At one level, the kind of anarchic experimentation with language seems remote from the kind of Romantic poetry for which the Lake District is famous.

If one keeps going east on the road that passes the Merzbarn it takes one into the beautiful Great Langdale Valley. Just over half a mile from the site of the Merzbarn is the Baysbrown Farm Campsite, a typical site of a sort found all over the Lake District. During most of the summer, the fields on the valley floor are given over to neatly arranged tents and camper vans. It was here that some of the Islamic terrorists involved in the London bombings on 7 July 2005 stayed in order to set up their training camp. Though this was not the only rural site at which such camps were operational, it seemed particularly incongruous that such activities should take place in the Lake District, the heart of English Romanticism.

Schwitters can be described as a terrorist in the sense defined by literary theorist Jean Paulhan. For Paulhan, writers since the eighteenth century have been trying to overcome the supposed inadequacy of literature and language to represent thought by demanding purity of expression shorn of the flowers of rhetoric. He explicitly compares this to the Terror of the French Revolution. Among the writers he cites are Apollinaire, Fargue and Eluard, whose 'secret desire is to humiliate language – sometimes to renew it, but always feeling they are worth more than it'.[7] Schwitters was one of a number of figures in the late nineteenth and early twentieth centuries who seemed determined to push the possibilities of poetic language and to explode its status as a source and vehicle of meaning and sense. Others working in a similar manner include Tristan Tzara, Guillaume Apollinaire and Velimir Khlebnikov. At its most extreme, such work can be extremely challenging, pushing the reader's or listener's capacity for making sense out of what they read or hear to the limit. But, despite what might seem an eschewal of meaning making, such work can be seen as an attempt to return poetry to a primal language of being, before Babel, what is called in German 'Ursprache', originary speech.

That Schwitters and the 7/7 terrorists both found themselves in the Lakes, the centre of English Romanticism, has a certain fitness. It can be argued that terrorism itself is a Romantic notion, which emerged in the French Revolution. Wordsworth famously both witnessed and celebrated the Revolution, at least to begin with, memorably declaring in his poem, 'French Revolution as it appeared to its enthusiasts at its commencement', 'Bliss was it in that dawn to be alive/But to be young was very heaven'.[8] He was, however, repelled by the Terror itself. For some commentators, contemporary Islamic terrorism has less to do with Islamic culture and theology, and more to do with the radical strain of Western revolutionary Romantic nihilism that is initiated by the French Revolution, and continues through Hitler, Stalin and other extreme exemplars. Simon Critchley, for example, talks of the 'Islamo-Jacobinism' of Al Qaeda, a comparison echoed by political theorist John Gray. Inasmuch as Romanticism was concerned with the reconfiguration of culture, and the overthrow of established norms, it can be seen to be, to a certain extent, a precursor of both the artistic avant-garde and terrorism. In particular, the Romantic concern with the sublime as a source of terror resonates with the very aims of terrorism itself.

Grange-over-Sands

Directly south of the Lake District is Morecambe Bay, which, on a map at least, resembles nothing more than a great chunk bitten out of the side of North West England, from Fleetwood in the south to Walney Island in the north. If one were to follow its coastal perimeter from south to north, starting at Fleetwood, one would pass the flat marshlands around Knott End-on-Sea, Cockerham, Glasson Dock and Sunderland Point, and then the modernist block of Heysham Nuclear Power Station, the village of Heysham itself, Morecambe, around the 'Area of Outstanding Natural Beauty' between Arncliffe and Silverdale, and then past the Cumbrian peninsula, and the retirement villages such as Grange-over-Sands, finally reaching Walney Island at the other end. One of the reasons that the Bay is so odd is that it seems to be always in an indeterminate state between land and sea, never quite being one or the other.

We first got to know the area properly when we lived in a village not far from Arnside, and would go for walks around Jenny Brown's Point, the strange outcropping of rock and beach on the side of the Bay. There was always something a little melancholy about these walks. This was emphasised by the sight of the two-carriage train, which we nicknamed 'Sad Train', slowly crossing the rail viaduct at Arnside and passing round the Bay at the opposite side of the River Kent, at one point disappearing into woods, towards the Cumbrian coast, including Sellafield.

One of the strange aspects of the Bay's shallowness is the colour of the sea/mud/sand (hard to know how else to put it), with its channels running across each other. Its dull, silver sheen always reminds me of pewter, that peculiar alloy made of tin which has been mixed with small amounts of other metals such as copper, lead or antimony to harden it and make it more durable. In turn, this reminds me of the famous mystical experience Jacob Boehme had in 1600 in which 'his eyes fell upon a burnished pewter dish, which reflected the sunshine with such marvellous splendor that he fell into an inward ecstasy, and it seemed to him as if he could now look into the principles and deepest foundations of things'.[1] Perhaps this connection is less perverse than it seems. For Rachel Carson, the edge of the sea, the shore, is 'the primeval meeting place of the elements of the earth and water, a place of compromise and conflict and eternal change'.[2]

The idea that the Bay is a strange place is shared by the novelist Andrew Michael Hurley, who set his debut novel, *The Loney*, in a lightly fictionalised version of the Bay. In an interview with the *Weird Fiction Review*, he describes Silverdale as 'a very strange, quiet place. The lanes are overhung with oaks and beeches and the woods full of ancient yew trees that split great spines of limestone'. But he is most interested in the coastline around the Bay, which has 'a reputation for being a dangerous place and the whole place is riddled with channels that shift and collapse after each tide. It's capricious and unknowable, a place to avoid'. He describes the place 'as being "primed" in some way, as though something was always about to happen—and it seemed very much like that'. Every time he went there he would find something new, something unexpected – 'a path through the woods that I hadn't noticed before, a meadow where no one ever went. It's a place that hasn't really moved on very much. It's still very old. It could be any time there. Anything could happen'.[3]

Anything could happen, anything can befall us. In his essay on the nature of language, Heidegger suggests that 'to undergo an experience with something – be it a thing, a person, or a god – means that this something befalls us, strikes us, comes over us, overwhelms and transforms us'.[4] For Heidegger, the poet undergoes an experience in language. Perhaps writing is always something that befalls, whether as writers or readers. Writing seems, to me at least, to involve a considerable degree of contingency, of chance, accident. Writing is perhaps both an artefact of the trauma of the contingency of our lives, and its possible cure, or in other words a *pharmakon*. Trauma comes from the Greek for wound. A wound is something that issues from an encounter with something other than us. It is the opening, the exposure of the inside to the outside.

This is perhaps why the title of Jenn Ashworth's novel *Fell*, which is set around the Bay, is so apt. The Bay is, as Hurley says, a place where anything can happen, where anything can befall us. The word *fell* is the past tense of the verb *to fall*, which comes from Old English *fællan* (Mercian), fyllan (West Saxon) 'make fall, cause to fall', also 'strike down, demolish, kill', from Proto-Germanic *falljan* 'strike down, cause to fall'. It is also a Cumbrian term for a hill derived from the Old Norse fiall 'mountain', from Proto-Germanic *felzam-* 'rock'. However, are these two meanings somehow connected, in that rocks fall?

I had promised myself to buy a copy of *Fell* only when it came out in paperback. This is partly out of meanness and partly because I far prefer paperbacks. By chance, however, I found a paperbound proof copy in the Oxfam bookshop in Gower Street in London. It was indeed chance that it was a proof copy, and not an advanced reader copy, as it contained an unintentional artefact that had escaped being edited out. About two-thirds down page 229 the following 'word' appears – 'Hhhhdkjgjg'.[5] This is not a word in any language as far as I can tell, or at least not yet. Despite this, I could decide to try to make sense of it in the context of the book. Perhaps it is intended as some kind of onomatopoeia, of throat clearing perhaps, even though the passage in question is a kind of indirect account of the thoughts and actions of one of the characters. However, such an interpretative puzzling is unnecessary as Ashworth herself has told me that this strange string of letters is, in fact, an artefact of her cat's interaction with the keyboard of the computer on which the book was being written. All of the letters in the string are next to each other on a standard QWERTY keyboard, with the exception of D which is separated from the others by F. How the cat missed the F is a bit of a mystery. (I imagine the cat pouncing on, falling on the keyboard.)

To encounter an artefact such as 'Hhhhdkjgjg' is unusual, even in a proof copy, and jarring. It produces a rent or tear, a wound or hole perhaps, in the diegetic, space–time continuum of the book's world. Its meaninglessness and unpronounceability foreground the materiality of the book itself, its composition of printed words and paper. Perhaps this is appropriate. In an email about her current writing, Ashworth writes that 'There are a lot of holes in my essays – sinkholes and earthquakes and windows and gunshot wounds – and they're all ways of thinking about what writing is – I call it "a trepanning" at one point – though whether the writer trepans the reader (so we're a violent, nasty, aggressive lot) or herself (a performance of self harm) I have not decided.'

This reminds me of a poem quoted by Kenneth Goldsmith in his book *Uncreative Writing*, by L=A=N=G=U=A=G=E poet Charles Bernstein:

HH/ ie,s obVrsxr;atjrn dugh seineocpcy i iibalfmgmMw er "me"ius ieigorcy¢jeuvine+pee.)a/nat" ihl"n,s ortnsihcldseløøpitemoBruce-oOiwv ewaa39osoanfJ++,r"P.[6]

This turns out to be 'a transcription of everything lifted off a page of correction tape from a manual typewriter.'[7] Goldsmith describes this as a kind of 'ghost writing.' Such a phrase is appropriate for Fell, which is a ghost story, with a haunted house at its centre.

Writing is always about the 'eerie.' When I was in the middle of writing this book, the blogger, writer and theorist Mark Fisher (also known as k-punk) tragically committed suicide. The last book he published shortly before his death was *The Weird and Eerie*. In it he distinguishes between the two eponymous terms, so apparently similar. Both are to do with the outside, but, for Fisher, the weird is 'something that *does not belong*. The weird brings to the familiar something which ordinarily lies beyond it, and which cannot be reconciled with the "homely"', the '*heimlich*' and thus is '*unheimlich*', uncanny, in Freud's terms. Thus, the most appropriate form for the weird is the montage, such as used by Surrealists in their juxtaposition of heterogeneous elements.[8] The eerie is also to do with the outside, but in a more literal sense. The eerie, unlike the weird, is not to be found in 'enclosed and inhabited domestic spaces' but rather in, for example, 'landscapes partially emptied of the human'. These lead us to ask, 'What happened to produce this ruin, this disappearance? What kind of entity was involved? What kind of thing was it that emitted such an *eerie cry*?'. Above all, for Fisher, the eerie 'entails a disengagement from our current attachments' though without the shock typical of the weird. There is a serenity in the eerie, as expressed in the phrase 'eerie calm', that is to do with 'detachment from the urgencies of the everyday'.[9] It can give us access to both those forces that govern the everyday but are obscured, and spaces beyond mundane reality altogether.

In *Fell*, Jack and Netty are ghosts haunting their old house, which has been recently reclaimed by their daughter Annette, after the death of her stepmother. The novel takes place both in the present day of the adult Netty and in her 1960s childhood as both she and her spectral parents remember it. All of them engage in recalling the presence in the house of the strange shamanic figure of Timothy Richardson, Tim, who seems to have the gift of healing and even of bringing the dead back to life, though he fails to cure the dying Netty.

The characters in *Fell* are human and non-human, living and non-living, organic and inorganic. Jack and Netty appear both as their younger living selves and as ghosts haunting the house inherited by their daughter Annette. The house itself is a central character. The division between life and death is continuously breached, not just in the form of ghosts, but also the bringing back to life of dead animals by the mercurial Tim. Another character, one which seems almost literally peripheral, but I suggest is of great importance, is the Bay itself.

Early on in *Fell*, Tim notices that Grange had, 'along with all the other little towns and fishing villages along this part of the coast, facing out to sea, an obsession with death'.[10] He is 'warned portentously about the mud and tides' and '[T]old gruesome stories about horses and carts being sucked into the quicksand, decapitated by the ropes meant to rescue them', as well as the lost women and children, maybe suicides, maybe drowned, the fishermen whose tractors 'had clapped out before the bore came in' who 'spent their last minutes wishing they'd stuck to the old ways and the horse and cart'.[11] As Tim puts it, 'the sands were a right bone yard'.[12]

At times, this has been literally true. In 1927, high seas led to ninety coffins being washed out to the bay from the graveyard of St Peters Church in Heysham. The bones had to be recovered, identified and reburied. The same graveyard has a memorial to the 2006 Morecambe Bay helicopter crash, in which seven men died, two pilots and five crewmen for the North Morecambe gas platforms.

Later on, the ghostly Jack and Netty, who speak and think together as 'we', ponder the 'dangerous and unpredictable' nature of the Bay, which 'changes daily', a reason for its 'siren charm, and danger of the edgelands'.[13] 'The gullies and channels shift, the sands run like mercury: no one can trace the same path across them twice'.[14] Over the course of the book's chronology the landscape is transformed. What was a beach when Jack and Netty were alive and living in Grange is now salt marsh, and their ghostly selves 'gaze, without recognition, on a landscape transformed'. This is because the River Kent, which flows into the Bay at Grange, 'is on the move', and will continue to migrate slowly south and away from the town, choking the beach up with silt, and making it disappear under 'a harsh scruff of spartina grass'.[15] 'There's nothing to be done about it' 'we' thinks. It is the nature of all deep water channels to be cyclical; to go where the wind takes them'.[16] 'But' we considers, 'one day the wind will turn again and when it does Kent will remember itself and advance on the marsh to drown the cordgrass. After the spring tide new channels will emerge overnight and turn the sea-washed turf into a treacherous maze of unmapped islands, slippery knolls and sucking mudflats.'[17] That Grange now looks over salt marsh rather than sea is eerie. There is an esplanade that runs above the marsh for a quite a distance, and which makes little sense until one remembers that it once faced out onto the sea.

The ghosts of Jack and Netty also haunt the lives of Eve and Maddy, and their son Jack, another set of contemporary characters, and accompany them on a walk across the Bay in the company of the 'bloke employed to guide them over the sands', who is not named in the book, but who anyone who lives in Cumbria will know to be Cedric Robinson, the Queen's Guide to the Sands.[18] Soon after we first arrived in the North West we went on one of these walks. About halfway, Cedric grew doubtful about the movement of water, and we had to turn back. It was only a few years after the deaths in 2004 of twenty-one undocumented Chinese migrant workers, employed illegally by a father-and-son team of gangmasters to pick cockles. The leader of the group had made a mistake about the time of the tides, and, despite being warned by English cocklers, most of the Chinese workers did not manage to get to shore.

Jack and Netty describe the process by which the pilot marks the way with laurel branches stuck into the sand, called 'brobs', and the 'nearly biblical' sight of 'two hundred or so followers across the rippled grey sand, barefoot, loaded with a battered rucksack and armed with a wooden staff as tall as he was.'[19] The brobs are to make sure the crowd of followers will keep on track and not fall into the quicksand, which he shows them, 'standing on the wobbling skin of the earth until the dun-coloured surface began to bend and buckle, so saturated with water it showed signs of cracking wide open, falling into crumbling fissures that would set and ooze without warning.'[20] When they reach Kent's Bank on the other side of the Bay, the pilot tells stories of the Bay.

'Distance means nothing out here; it's flat, it plays tricks on you. It might as well be the surface of the moon. I can read these sands like you could open up a newspaper in the morning and read that,' he said, 'but they say something different every day. The tide comes in, and a few hours later, when it drops off, it carves patterns in the flats. You'd never get sick of it.'[21]

The Bay is, perhaps, a figure for writing itself. It is neither the maternal, liquid ocean in which we might dissolve, nor the solid land of delineated things, facts and concepts. It is rather a liminal space on the edge of both, continually inscribed and reinscribed, a perilous space where everything keeps changing and through which we have to find our way among the ghosts of those who have failed to do so.

Ribblesdale

Writing about Walter Benjamin, Jacques Derrida suggests that ruins are not a negative, or even a thing at all. He expresses a wish to write a small treatise on the love of ruins. 'One cannot love a monument, a work of architecture, an institution as such except in an experience itself precarious in its fragility: it hasn't always been there, it will not always be there, it is finite.'[1] I love the landscape of Cumbria, where I live, and that love is bound up with the image, the imagination, of its ruin. I imagine the land made desolate by some catastrophe, a nuclear holocaust perhaps, or an ecological disaster, or simply the inexorable passage of time. By chance, at home I came across a book my daughter had bought, called *The Death of Grass*, by John Christopher. Published in 1956, it is now regarded as a classic of dystopian and apocalyptic science fiction. It is set in what was then the near future, at a time when a virus is destroying all forms of grass, including cereal crops, presaging famine on a global scale. By the time the main section of the novel starts, this has already caused social and political turmoil in the Far East. The main protagonist, John Custance, an architect, hears from a friend working for the government that there is a plan to destroy London and other population centres with atomic and nuclear bombs, to reduce the populace sufficiently so that the survivors might be fed. Most of the novel is concerned with the journey undertaken by Custance, his family, friends and associates, from London to his brother's farm in Westmorland, or what is now Cumbria.

The brother has anticipated the coming of the virus to Britain, and barricaded the only entrance to the valley in which his farm sits. Though the government is overthrown before the plan to bomb the cities can be carried out, all forms of order collapse and Christopher is concerned to show how, with the overthrow of authority and the loss of normality, even the most apparently civilised people become violent and barbaric. Christopher is not a particularly lyrical writer, and much of the book is given to dialogue, or terse description to move the plot along. Nevertheless, occasional glimpses are given of the landscape as it is transformed by both the ecological and social consequences of the virus. I find these passages strangely alluring as they offer a vision of the North West of England so at odds with the visions of rural idyll peddled by the tourist industry.

The western approach to Garsdale had been through a narrow strip of good grazing land which now, in the steady rain, was a band of mud, studded here and there with farm buildings. They looked down to Sedbergh, resting between hills and valley on the other side of the Rawthey. Smoke lay above it, and drifted westwards along the edge of the moors. Sedbergh was burning.[2]

A little later, the group see evidence of the changing values brought about by the crisis:

They moved down into the valley, passing the signs of destruction, which had been evident from higher up but which here were underlined in brutal scoring. What refugees there were avoided them; they had no temptation to look to an armed band for help. Near the ruins of Sedbergh they saw a group, of about the same number as their own, emerging from the town. The women were wearing what looked like expensive jewellery, and one of the men was carrying pieces of gold plate. Even while John watched, he threw some of it away as being too heavy. Another man picked it up, weighed it in his hand, and dropped it again with a laugh. They went on, keeping to the east of John's band, and the gold remained, gleaming dully against the brown grassless earth.[3]

The next paragraph gives a chilling sense of complete social breakdown.

From an isolated farm-house, as they struck up towards the valley of the Lune, they heard a screaming, high-pitched and continuous, that unsettled the children and some of the women. There were two or three men lounging outside the farm-house with guns. John led his band past, and the screams faded into the distance.[4]

Further in their journey, what was once shocking becomes normal.

The moors had been more or less deserted, but when they descended to cross the lower land north of Kendal, they witnessed the signs, by now familiar, of the predatory animal that man had become: houses burning, an occasional cry in the distance that might be either of distress or savage exultance, the sights and sounds of murder. And another of their senses was touched — here and there their nostrils were pricked by the sour-sweet smell of flesh in corruption.[5]

In 1970, the book was filmed under its American title, *No Blade of Grass*. Directed by Cornel Wilde, it takes some liberties with the original plot, updating the action to the later 1970s (then again the near future), and altering some of the characters and their relationships. The film is very much an artefact of its time, with its quotidian acting and filming and the occasional, rather unconvincing, attempt at avant-garde use of colour. There are some nice touches, including a biker gang, with Viking horns on their helmets who could have come out of the first Mad Max film, one or two shots that are almost worthy of Tarkovsky, and a great image of an abandoned Rolls-Royce. It wears its ecological conscience on its sleeve. The first five minutes are a series of images of pollution and crowds, culminating in two shots of nuclear bomb explosions. Interestingly, between Christopher's book and the film new forms of environmental consciousness have emerged; a schoolboy character in the film gives an explanation of what we now call 'global warming'. What makes it fascinating for me is that much of the action takes place on location in the valley that runs between the peaks of Whernside and Ingleborough. The director makes particularly good use of the Ribblehead Viaduct, a 400-metre-long arched structure that takes the railway across Batty Moss.

It is obvious that the viaduct is being used in *No Blade of Grass* for its visual impact, rather than any relation it might have to the broader themes the film might have. Yet there is a direct connection between the concern with global warming and general ecological catastrophe that pervades the film, and the viaduct. The Settle to Carlisle railway line, built between 1869 and 1875, was one of the last of the great engineering projects of the Victorian era to rely upon the labour of navvies, before the advent of the mechanical digger. As such, it is part of what McKenzie Wark calls the 'carbon liberation' that has ushered in the era of the Anthropocene.[6] What is perhaps particularly eerie is that the devastation that the film projects into the near future has, in some ways, already happened. The land around the viaduct appears undisturbed, other than by the many walkers who come to this part to enjoy the experience of what they believe to be its unspoilt nature.

In *The Railway Navvies*, one of the few books on the subject, Terry Coleman describes the extraordinary difficulty of building a railway in this harsh terrain. In these 'bleak and wild moors' there 'wasn't a level piece of ground between' Settle and Carlisle, according to one farmer.[7] What Coleman describes as the 'two horrors' of the line were bog and boulder clay. The navvies had to use 'bog carts' which ran on barrels. Normal cartwheels would have sunk up to the axles. Coleman quotes an engineer who often witnessed bog carts 'hauled over the moss by three horses, till they sank up to their middles and had to be drawn out one at a time by their necks to save their lives.'[8] The clay was so hard it had to be drilled and blasted, but after rain it turned into a 'gluey mess.' The navvies hated it, especially when they struck what they took to be soft clay with their picks and struck a boulder as hard as iron.[9] In these conditions it took four and a half years to build Swardale Viaduct alone. Many navvies found the conditions intolerable, with the ground that could go from hard rock to soup in an instant, and the incessant rain – ninety-two inches in Dent Head in 1872, compared to twenty-five in London – so the working population was especially transient, even in relation to other similar rail projects.[10] Though there were only 1,700 to 2,000 navvies working at a time on the line, 33,000 worked in total over the six years. The rain in particular caused endless problems. Works just melted in the face of its onslaught. At one point, a cutting was made and rails laid, which was then buried overnight. Two years later, while making another gullet, the original rails were rediscovered. Coleman quotes an engineer: 'A splendid discovery for a geological fellow. He could prove lots from this. Here is a railway in the glacial drift, in the glacial period, rails, sleepers and all. Then the world must have been inhabited then; and they had railways then; there is nothing new under the sun'.[11]

What makes the construction of this particular stretch of the Settle to Carlisle line so fascinating is that its remoteness necessitated the building of shanty towns, five in all, named Sebastopol (after the navvies' contribution to the Crimean War), Batty Green or Batty Wife Hold, Belgravia, where the viaduct chiefs may have lived, and where the houses had porches and double skins (thus why it is named after a smart part of London), Inkerman, another name from the Crimean War, Jordan, Jericho and Jerusalem, as well as other more remote settlements. There were also shops, a post office, pubs, a public library, a mission, a hospital and a 'dead house'. Of all this there is nothing left.

Sunderland Point

Sunderland Point is a small village on a spit of land located where the River Lune issues out into Morecambe Bay. Though not far from Lancaster, it feels remote for a number of reasons. To get there from Lancaster requires driving out towards Morecambe on the A683, a road notorious for its congestion, and then turning left on the B5273, past the big Asda store and the Salt Ayre leisure centre on the left, and the sprawling White Lund industrial estate on the right. This is one of the most dispiriting landscapes in this part of the North West, a massive accumulation of anonymous sheds containing car dealerships, light industrial units, van rental companies, scrapyards and storage facilities, connected by a confusing array of small roads. In the First World War, White Lund had been the site of the National Filling Factory, opened by the Ministry of Munitions in 1916, to fill shell cases. Presumably it was the remote nature of the area that led to the factory being located there. On 1 October 1917, a massive explosion at the factory killed ten people and was heard as far away as Burnley.

At the roundabout, the first exit takes the visitor away from the estate and into the quiet and somewhat eerie marshy land beyond. You pass through small, largely undistinguished villages, such as Heaton and Overton, largely consisting of one or two older houses surrounded by bungalows and postwar houses, presumably intended mostly for the retired. Eventually the road to Sunderland Point is reached by crossing a cattle grid. Here there is a stark warning:

DANGER
Beware of fast tides hidden channels
and quick sands

On the road itself there is a further notice, this time in white on red:

DANGER
do not proceed if these posts are in water

This makes Sunderland Point unique, apparently, in being the only part of the United Kingdom that is on the mainland but to which access is limited by tides. The road, when it is passable, still bears the evidence of being inundated, with moisture and sand strewn across it even on the driest day. It passes through a landscape of grey mud marsh, covered in dirty-looking grass and cut with deep inlets, often half full of water. Sunderland Point itself is reached from a beach, which is also the only place for visitors to park. The village is little more than a row of houses, some quite elegant along a quayside. Though they all appear to be private residences, there is a sense that once some of the buildings had other purposes, pubs perhaps or even customs houses. At the end of the point, one of the houses, complete with veranda, resembles a plantation house from the antebellum south of the United States, an apt comparison as it turns out. All the houses face across the Lune to Glasson Dock, the farmlands around it and Lancaster.

About halfway along the line of houses, there is a road running inland across the point with a few more houses. After about a hundred yards, after the last house, it turns into a narrow footpath, which passes a mission church. At the end of the footpath you find yourself on a very narrow rocky strip of grass and sand, and a considerable amount of debris of one sort or another. Beyond that there is more marshland, this time leading to the sea. To your right, the cube shape of Heysham Nuclear Power Station sits ominously.

If you turn to your left and walk along the narrow strip of land, within about fifty feet you come to a small area of grass with steps up to it. Here is one of the most fascinating sights in this part of Lancashire, Sambo's Grave. This is the unconsecrated ground in which a young slave, who had recently arrived in England and died

of a disease to which he probably had no immunity, was buried in
1736. The grave remained unmarked and anonymous until 1796,
when a local poet decided to commemorate him by composing
a poem which was then engraved on a metal plate, which was
attached to the stone

Here Lies

Poor SAMBOO

A faithful NEGRO

Who

(Attending his Master from the West Indies)

DIED on his Arrival at SUNDERLAND

Full sixty Years the angry Winter's Wave

Has thundering dashed this bleak and barren Shore

Since SAMBO's head laid in this lonely GRAVE

Lies still and ne'er will hear their turmoil more.

Full many a Sand-bird chirps upon the Sod,

And many a Moonlight Elfin round him trips

Full many a Summer's Sunbeam warms the Clod

And many a teeming Cloud upon him drips.

But still he sleeps – till the awakening Sounds,

Of the Archangel's Trump new Life impart,

Then the GREAT JUDGE his Approbation founds,

Not on Man's COLOR but his WORTH of HEART

Sambo's presence at Sunderland is a reminder that the area
was once part of the triangular trade in which slaves were taken
from Africa to the United States and the Caribbean. The goods
such as molasses those slaves helped produce were brought to
Britain and Europe and could be distilled as rum, the profits from
which could be used to buy manufactured goods to be exported
to Africa, and more slaves bought to be taken to the United States
and the Caribbean, and so on. The voyage made by the slaves to
the New World, almost always in appalling conditions, was called

the 'middle passage'. For Paul Gilroy, it is the hybridity of identity that emerges out of the slaves' experience of diaspora in what he calls the 'Black Atlantic' that creates modern black identity.[1]

Sunderland Point was developed by the Quaker Robert Lawson as a small port servicing the triangular trade in the early eighteenth century. (The Quaker involvement with slavery is one of the less edifying parts of its history, despite being one of the first religious groups to denounce it.) It was built out of stone from the eerie Cockersands Abbey on the other side of the Lune. Shifting tides and sands, and the building of bigger ports at Glasson Dock and Lancaster, led to the decline of Sunderland and to Lawson's bankruptcy. Nevertheless, it is an important part of the North West's contribution to the grim history of the slave trade. In the later eighteenth century, Lancaster itself became the fourth major slave port in Britain, after Liverpool, London and Bristol, with Whitehaven, up the coast, not far behind. Because Lancaster was a river port rather than a seaport the ships it received were smaller, and thus aimed at different trade routes and markets than the others. Lancaster merchants tended to buy slaves from smaller markets and be more adventurous than Whitehaven merchants in where they sold them, often in mainland America rather than Jamaica and Barbados. It was this that enabled Lancaster to continue as a slave port after Whitehaven had more or less given up in response to Liverpool's increasing dominance.

When writing or reading accounts such as these, it is tempting to see slavery as something unfortunate but safely in the past. However, it is worth remembering how much of what we value in our Western culture is bound up with the world made possible by slavery. Both Whitehaven and Lancaster are full of Georgian buildings seemingly exemplifying the values of neoclassicism, the enlightenment and rationalism, and at the same time being direct results of the prosperity bought about by the slave trade.

Slavery also remains central to our culture for deeper and more complex reasons. Though it may not, technically, exist, in the developed world at least, it still informs the very notion of what it is to be human. The fate of poor Sambo offers a clue to why this is. Here is an account of his death from the *Lonsdale Magazine*, written by 'J T' of Kendal in 1822.

After she had discharged her cargo, he was placed at the inn… with the intention of remaining there on board wages till the vessel was ready to sail; but supposing himself to be deserted by the master, without being able, probably from his ignorance of the language, to ascertain the cause, he fell into a complete state of stupefaction, even to such a degree that he secreted himself in the loft on the brewhouses and stretching himself out at full length on the bare boards refused all sustenance. He continued in this state only a few days, when death terminated the sufferings of poor Samboo [sic]. As soon as Samboo's exit was known to the sailors who happened to be there, they excavated him in a grave in a lonely dell in a rabbit warren behind the village, within twenty yards of the sea shore, whither they conveyed his remains without either coffin or bier, being covered only with the clothes in which he died.[2]

Thus, it seems that Sambo did not merely die of some disease but actively sought his own death, or perhaps regarded himself as in some senses already dead in the absence of his master. This is how Orlando Patterson conceives of slavery in his groundbreaking work *Slavery and Social Death*. For Patterson, slavery involves far more than the mere operations of power, or of the instrumentalisation of one human being by another, but instead is based on a particular status given to the slave, that of social death. He also shows that slavery is neither primarily necessarily about labour or about profit. It is instead about 'the permanent violent domination of natally alienated and generally dishonoured persons'.[3] For Patterson the unbearable contradictions of enslaving another human being are resolved by regarding them as dead, at least in social terms. He views slavery as 'a highly symbolized domain of human experience'.[4] He takes his cue about how this symbolisation works from the ethnographic research of Claude

Meillassoux and Michel Izard, who characterise the process of slavery in terms of a number of transitional phases, including being uprooted from his or her own milieu, and incorporated into that of the master, but as a 'nonbeing', or an unborn being (*non-né*), this leading to the slave's 'social death'.[5]

Patterson thinks this overemphasises the coercive nature of enslavement, and fails to take account of cases of local recruitment of slaves. He distinguishes between those slaves who come from the outside, or what he calls the 'intrusive' mode, and those from the inside, the 'extrusive'. What characterises the intrusive incorporation of the slave into the master's milieu is his or her status as 'the permanent enemy on the inside', without an ancestral home or place in the cosmos.[6] Those who become slaves from within a particular society are regarded as having fallen from normal participation in a community'.[7] In either case this meant that they were socially dead, the 'living dead'. It was in this social death that the master's power resided, because it was he who 'mediated between the socially dead and the socially alive'. The slave was also important in that his or her own marginality and anomalousness 'emphasized what was important and stable'.[8] In a fascinating reading of the Anglo-Saxon poem *Beowulf*, Patterson points to the fact that the person who can lead Beowulf to the dragon is a slave, but this person is not counted among the twelve men who go to the dragon's den. The slave can 'lead Beowulf across the deadly margin that separated the social order above from the terror and chaos of the underground, between good and evil, between the sacred world of the Christian and the profane world of the Pagan' 'precisely because he was marginal, neither human nor inhuman, neither man nor beast, neither dead nor alive, the enemy within who was neither member nor true alien'.[9]

Thus, 'the essence of slavery is that the slave, in his social death, lives on the margin between community and chaos, life and death, the sacred and the secular. Already dead, he lives outside the mana of the gods and can cross the boundaries with social and supernatural impunity'.[10] However, Patterson is careful to show that slavery did not involve taboos about pollution that characterise caste systems. This is because the relation between slave and master was so close, involving sexual relations and suckling for example, which would make the ritual avoidance and segregation of caste unworkable and contradictory. The relation of personal domination between master and slave resulted in a 'perverse intimacy' in which the 'slave's only life was through and for his master'.[11] This would explain Sambo's death as something more complex than the result of disease. It is as if, without his master, he ceased to be alive, or rather, to be a member of the living dead, animated only by his master's presence.

Patterson describes the complex rituals and marks of enslavement that enabled the process of becoming socially dead, including symbolic rejection of the slave's own natal culture, and initiation into the master's culture, branding or the shaving of part or all of the hair, and the assumption of 'fictive kinship' between master and slave.[12] (Fascinatingly, Patterson suggests that the most important distinguishing aspect of an African slave was not skin colour, but hair, which is far more racially determined.[13]) Also of great importance is renaming; the giving of slave names, often barely distinguishable from the names of cattle. Some of these names became shorthand for the way slaves were regarded. Patterson describes the 'ideology of Sambo', as representing for the southern plantation owner the epitome of the 'degraded man-child'. He quotes Stanley Elkins, who defines the image of Sambo, 'the typical plantation slave' as 'docile but irresponsible, loyal but lazy, humble but chronically given to lying and stealing... full of infantile silliness and his talk inflated with childish exaggeration'. It is this childishness that makes him 'both exasperating and lovable'.[14]

The North was haunted by the disavowed black body of the slave. Unlike in the United States, in which slaves were a vital part of the agricultural economy, especially in the South, England generally kept its slave labour 'off-shore' in the Caribbean. Slaves were kept in England, albeit in small numbers. Among the more notorious instances of slave ownership in the North West is that of the Sills family in Dentdale. Dentdale is an extraordinary remote valley in Eastern Cumbria, surrounded by bare moorland, but itself verdant and lush, like a kind of Cumbrian Shangri-la. It is still comparatively inaccessible and must have been extremely difficult to get to in the eighteenth and nineteenth centuries, and even up to the building of the M6 in the 1960s. The Sills lived in High Rigg farmhouse on Whernside, one of the 'three peaks' of what is now North Yorkshire. They made enough money from owning slave ships to move to the grander West House in Dentdale. It is known that they kept slaves, owing to an advertisement in a Liverpool Paper placed by Edmond Sill of Dent, offering a reward for the return of an escaped black slave, Thomas Anson, 'a Negro Man, about five feet six inches high, aged 20 years or upwards'. There are a number of rumours concerning the Sills and slavery; that the local river the Black Dub is so named because this is where the slaves would wash themselves; that a female slave was drowned in the Dub; that a tunnel runs from Rigg End Farm to Whernside Manor; and that West House, or Whernside Manor as it is now called, has chains for restraining slaves in its cellars (though none has been found). There is also supposedly a burial ground for slaves in Dent, though that too has not been found.

More complicatedly there are a number of stories concerning Anne Sills, who inherited all the Sills' land and houses in the early nineteenth century. One concerned her relationship with Richard Sutton, a foundling her father had brought back to Dent but had bought up with the slaves, despite him being white. Sutton rose to be the estate manager, and Anne must have been fond of him, despite having him flogged at one point, as she left him High Rigg, and one-tenth of her income in her will. Another is that Anne fell in love with a black coachman, who was then murdered by her brothers, to prevent an inappropriate liaison. A skeleton has been found under the flagstones of Whernside House, so this may be true. It has been suggested, firstly by local historian Kim Lyon, that these stories became known to Charlotte Brontë when she attended Cowan Bridge School, which is very close to Dent.[15] It is thought that she may have conflated the story of Sutton and Anne with that of the black coachman when writing *Wuthering Heights*. In the novel, Heathcliff is described as 'dark as though it came from the Devil'. In her 2011 film version, Andrea Arnold cast James Howson, a black actor, as Heathcliff. One irony of this casting is that Howson's voice was overdubbed.

In 1943, Eric Williams' groundbreaking work *Capitalism and Slavery* made the argument that the slave trade made the Industrial Revolution in England possible, which in turn led to the abolition of slavery.[16] For Williams, the enslaving of Africans was not in itself racist, but rather a purely economic decision, which in turn fostered modern racism. Slaves and indentured workers came from a variety of backgrounds in early modernity, including from within the slave-owning countries, but in the end the African slave proved to be the most fit for purpose. Slavery and the triangular trade produced both the capital and the infrastructure that supported the Industrial Revolution. The abolition of the slave trade was also less a question of humanity and more of economic necessity. Thus, slavery created the conditions of its own abolition by making the Industrial Revolution possible. Williams' thesis has been much debated since the publication of the book, and is even now still the subject of responses by historians. But if one accepts Williams' conclusions then it would seem that our modern world is built on the bodies of slaves, and this is particularly true of the North of England, with Liverpool as a slave port enabling the extraordinary development of modern industry in the area.

Yet, though industrialisation led to the end of slavery in the most literal sense, the slave became the model for the modern, industrial labourer. In *The Human Condition*, Hannah Arendt distinguishes between work and labour. The former is the province of *homo faber*, and the latter that of *animale laborans*, the exemplary figure of which is the slave. This is prefigured in Ruskin's distinction, in *The Nature of Gothic*, between the savage freedom of the Gothic craftsman, and the repetitive slavery of the classical artisan, and by implication the industrial worker.

But there is an irony here. The Industrial Revolution so vehemently opposed by Ruskin also offered the opportunity for its beneficiaries to put his ideas about architecture into practice. In his study *English Culture and the Decline of the Industrial Spirit 1850–1980*, historian Martin Wiener suggests that the apogee of the Industrial Revolution in the mid-nineteenth century was followed by a reaction against industrialisation by the very people who most benefitted. The newly rich whose money came from industrial enterprise rejected their entrepreneurial roots, and embraced an upper or at least upper-middle-class way of being. The sons of the industrialists were sent to the major public schools, or if not to their lesser imitators, and to the old universities, Oxford and Cambridge. They were encouraged to study the humanities and to eschew practical disciplines such as engineering, or indeed anything that might be construed as exhibiting a concern with business, making money and profit, or what was often characterised as Americanness. Central to this assumption of a kind of aristocratic lifestyle was the obsession with the rural, and an idealised vision of the English countryside as the heart of the nation. This in turn led to the building of houses for those enriched by the Industrial Revolution, which, in Wiener's words, looked 'as old as a new house could'.[17] He points out that '[L]and had ceased being a major source of wealth and the country house was now valued more as a symbol of ancestry than of economic power'. Thus, country houses 'now sought to blend into, rather than dominate the landscape'.[18] His example of this is C. F. A. Voysey's Broadleys, which is in the Lake District. Indeed, because of its comparatively cheap land, the Lake District was the ideal location to build such houses, and the area is indeed full of nineteenth- and early twentieth-century mansions for those newly rich hoping to appear as aristocrats. Such houses include Gatehouse, Brockhole, Blackwell, Cragwood, Langdale Chase, Moor Crag, Underley and Broadleys. Many are now hotels.

Grizedale

If the Lake District lacks great houses surrounded by rich agricultural land, the model of the homes of the so-called landed
gentry, it does however have many grand holiday homes built for
those made newly rich by industrialisation and other sources of
wealth that emerged in the nineteenth century. For example, Lake
Windermere boasts several of the most important Arts and Crafts
houses in Britain: Blackwell, Broadleys and Waterbeck. In Furness
Edwin Lutyens designed a guest house for Vickers Ltd.

It was in this context that the eminently Gothic Grizedale Hall
was built in 1905 for Harold Brocklebank, a director of his family
shipping line by the firm Walker, Carter and Walker of Windermere,
and, later, a director of the Cunard Line. Photographs of the
building show a robust, mock baronial mansion. It had been built
near the sites of earlier buildings, the first also known as Grizedale
Hall, and the second as Grizedale New Hall, with the former built
by the Rawlinson family in the early seventeenth century, and the
latter by Montague Ainslie in 1841, which was pulled down in 1904
to make way for Brocklebank's building.

Cunard had been started in 1839 by the Nova Scotian ship
owner Samuel Cunard as a response to the British government
tendering out contracts for steam packet services to run from
Britain to North America, specifically Liverpool to Halifax. By
the 1850s Cunard were carrying passengers in steamships across
the Atlantic from Liverpool to New York. It was trade that made
Cunard a wealthy company, and allowed them to take over rivals
such as the much older T and J Brocklebank.

Cunard, perhaps more than most other Liverpool shipping
firms, however, offers a rich symbol of the rise and fall of Liverpool
and thus of the shifting fortunes and reputation of the North West

of England. At about the same time the company was taking over firms such as Brocklebank it was also building its new headquarters at the Pier Head on the banks of the River Mersey. Started in 1914 and completed in 1917, it was designed by William Edward Willink and Philip Coldwell Thicknesse in a mixture of Italian Renaissance and Greek Revival style, resembling an Italian palace. Along with the Liver Building, headquarters of the Royal Liver Assurance company, and the Mersey Docks and Harbour Board Offices (now The Port of Liverpool Building), the Cunard Building was one of the so-called Three Graces of Liverpool, collectively representing the Edwardian wealth of the city and considerable confidence in its future.

Of course, as is well known, this confidence was ill founded. Liverpool was badly bombed in the Second World War, and then ineptly and only partially rebuilt afterward, and by the 1970s containerisation had made Liverpool's docks increasingly obsolete and its manufacturing industries were in steep decline, meaning that the city had one of the highest rates of unemployment in the country, and also considerable amounts of derelict land and buildings, as well as turbulent confrontations such as the Toxteth riots of 1981.

Grizedale Hall was lived in by Brocklebank and his family until his death in 1936, at which point it and the estate were acquired by the Forestry Commission. During the War it was requisitioned by the War Office and became the No 1 POW Camp (Officers) Grizedale Hall, for elite prisoners of war such as General Field Marshall Gerd von Rundstedt and U-boat captain Otto Kretschmer. But after the War, in 1957, the Forestry Commission decided that the house was too expensive to run, auctioned off the contents and demolished all but part of the terrace, which is now part of the car park for the visitors' centre.

A young man named Bill Grant joined the Forestry Commission in 1936, the year it acquired the Grizedale estate. After war service in the Far East he worked in Thornthwaite Forest in Cumbria. By 1963, he had been appointed head forester at Grizedale, where he was able to put into action ideas about how the forest could be made both richer in wildlife and more access-ible. He was encouraged in this by the man who had appointed him, Jack Chard, conservator of forests, North West England. Chard was concerned to overcome the resistance among foresters to allow the public into the forests, and his appointment of Grant was in aid of this. Grant introduced small lakes into the forests to attract mallards, teal and greylags, and oversaw the reintroduction of the pine marten, and of the capercaillie for the first time since the seventeenth century. This in turn attracted predators such as the golden eagle. He expanded the Deer Museum the Commission had set up in 1956 for the instruction of stalkers and other staff into a full-blown visitors' centre, in which the public could learn about the wildlife of the forest. This was an acknowledgement of the greater numbers of people coming to the forest, and therefore the increasing need to accommodate them, and to cater for the different kinds of visitors, from tourists to naturalists. In turn this required car parks, camp sites and forest walks, as well as the cre-ation of areas restricted to those involved in research projects on wildlife management.

That Grizedale Hall, built at the height of confidence in the Liverpool shipping trade, should be demolished at the beginning of the city's decline is perhaps symbolic of its changing fortunes, and of those of the North of England more generally. But it was also the moment when something else was just about to emerge in the city that would have momentous results. The psychoana-lyst Carl Jung is supposed to have predicted this in his famous 'Liverpool' dream which he experienced in 1927. In his account of this dream, he describes finding himself in a dirty, sooty city, at night, in winter and in the rain, which he knows to be Liverpool (despite never having visited it in reality). With his dream companions, a half-dozen fellow Swiss, he walks to the centre of 'a broad square dimly illuminated by street lights, into which many streets converged. The various quarters of the city were arranged radially around the square. In the center was a round pool, and in the middle of it a small island. While everything round about was obscured by rain, fog, smoke and dimly lit darkness, the little island blazed with sunlight. On it stood a single tree, a magnolia, in a shower of reddish blossoms. It was as though the tree stood in the sunlight and were at the same time the source of light.[1] His companions commented on the weather, without seeing the tree, while Jung 'was carried away by the beauty of the flowering tree and the sunlit island.[2] Jung comments on this dream as follows.

The dream represented my situation at the time. I can still see the grayish-yellow raincoats, glistening with the wetness of the rain. Everything was extremely unpleasant, black and opaque – just as I felt then. But I had a vision of unearthly beauty, and that is why I was able to live at all. Liverpool is the 'pool of life.' The 'liver,' according to an old view, is the seat of life, that which makes to live.[3]

Though Jung never visited Liverpool, and clearly it is the name that is important for him, many have been tempted to see his dream as prophetic of what happened in the city in the late 1950s and 1960s. Despite, or more likely because of its incipient decline, and also owing to its status as a port and its rich mixture of races and cultures, Liverpool always had a lively, albeit provincial, cultural scene. In 1957, the year Grizedale Hall was demolished, a young man called John Lennon formed a skiffle band in Liverpool with some school friends. Later that year, he met Paul McCartney, who joined the group. A year later, so did George Harrison. Over the next few years, this basic lineup was supplemented by various other players, while at the same time the group went by a number of different names. By 1960, they had become known as The Beatles, and in 1962 Ringo Starr joined as drummer. Despite being initially an American phenomenon in the 1950s, bands such as, pre-eminently, The Beatles had made England the centre of popular music culture. This in turn was massively aided by the art school education many young working-class people, including John Lennon, were able to enjoy because of the 1944 Education Act.

The story of The Beatles' extraordinary rise is well documented elsewhere. What is important here is their central role in the emergence of the counterculture, and in giving the North of England a role in that emergence. What is often underappreciated is the degree to which The Beatles in particular acted as a conduit between the artistic avant-garde and popular culture. Though it is fashionable to regard Lennon as the more forward looking in this regard, it was actually McCartney who was initially more active in finding out about radical art movements and ideas. It was he for example who was the first to listen to the music of Karlheinz Stockhausen. He had become involved in the counterculture while going out with Jane Asher, and living in her parents' house in central London. John Asher, Jane's brother, was involved in setting up an alternative bookshop and gallery with Barry Miles and John Dunbar (then Marianne Faithfull's husband). Named INDICA (after the Latin name for dope, *cannabis sativa forma indica*), it was funded in part by McCartney. The bookshop was a vital source for McCartney and others of alternative poetry, philosophy and thought, while the gallery showed work by artists involved in avant-garde art movements such as Kinetic Art, Op Art and Fluxus. Among those who showed at the gallery were Liliane Lijn, Takis, Mark Boyle and Joan Hills (the Boyle Family), and Yoko Ono. It was at that particular evening that John famously met Yoko, an encounter that has been much described, as well as its aftermath. What is more important, for this account at least, is the kind of art that was being shown.

Ono, for example, was a member of the extraordinarily important postwar art movement Fluxus, whose founders were among the attendees at John Cage's legendary sessions at the New School for Social Research, at which he engaged with the radical implications of his experiments at Black Mountain College in art as performance. Fluxus, as the name suggests, was greatly concerned with process. In this regard, it can be seen as part of the legacy of process thinking that extends back through Cage and the Black Mountain College and Charles Olson, its rector in the 1950s, to the original process philosophy of Alfred North Whitehead. Along with the postwar development of Cybernetics, such process thinking was vital for the development of environmentalism and ecological awareness.

Far earlier in the United States, Henry David Thoreau had famously advocated living simply in natural surroundings. In the mid-twentieth century, the West Coast of the United States, in particular northern California and San Francisco, was the location of avant-garde literary and artistic experimentation, by poets associated with the Black Mountain College, as well as those of the Beat Movement. Part of the ethos of this West Coast movement was a concern with ecological questions, and with rethinking how humans might relate to nature. This was influenced by Far Eastern ideas and phenomena, such as Zen Buddhism, Taoism and Chinese and Japanese literary traditions concerned with nature. Exemplary of this is the work of the poet and activist Gary Snyder, who combined ecological consciousness, first nation knowledge, Buddhism and a concern for the rural environment in his writings.

Such a combination can be seen as informing the development of land art or earth art, the movement that originated in the 1960s in which artists sought to make work that engaged with the landscape. Land art was first and foremost an American phenomenon, with the work of Alan Sonfist, Michael Heizer, Walter de Maria and others, with Robert Smithson as perhaps its most famous exponent. Smithson's best-known work, *Spiral Jetty*, is an exemplary piece of late 1960s land art, which involved dredging the Great Salt Lake in Utah, to produce a spiralling spit of land projecting into the lake, the visibility of which varies according to the water levels. *Spiral Jetty* is a confrontational work that required a number of dump trucks, a large tractor and other equipment to move over 6,500 tonnes of rock and earth into the lake. Smithson was also attracted by the harshness of the landscape and its lack of obvious rural beauty, and its industrial remains. Furthermore, the work is in part at least a comment on the Vietnam War.

Though land art was largely an American phenomenon it did boast a couple of important English representatives, most famously Richard Long, Hamish Fulton and Andy Goldsworthy. In 1967, at the age of twenty-two and while still a student at St Martins, Richard Long made a work of art that has since been recognised as of considerable importance in the development of what Rosalind Krauss would call 'sculpture in the expanded field.' He walked back and forth in a straight line in a grassy field in the English countryside and photographed the resulting track.

Nature has always been a subject of art, from the first cave paintings to twentieth-century landscape photography. I wanted to use the landscape as an artist in new ways. First I started making work outside using natural materials like grass and water, and this led to the idea of making a sculpture by walking. This was a straight line in a grass field, which was also my own path, going 'nowhere'. In the subsequent early map works, recording very simple but precise walks on Exmoor and Dartmoor, my intention was to make a new art which was also a new way of walking: walking as art. Each walk followed my own unique, formal route, for an original reason, which was different from other categories of walking, like travelling. Each walk, though not by definition conceptual, realised a particular idea. Thus walking – as art – provided a simple way for me to explore relationships between time, distance, geography and measurement. These walks are recorded in my work in the most appropriate way for each different idea: a photograph, a map, or a text work. All these forms feed the imagination.[4]

What is noteworthy about *A Line Made by Walking* and perhaps all of Long's work, as well as that of his fellow English land artist Andy Goldsworthy, is how their version of land art remains very English, and indeed part of a national tradition of pastoral art which can be traced back to the nineteenth century and before.

Unlike American artists such as Robert Smithson, there is little overt politics in their work. Nor do they ever stray from rural situations and a fairly essentialist understanding of 'nature'. As such they are in keeping with the contemporary development of ecological awareness in the late 1960s and early 1970s, which also cleaved to a fairly essentialist understanding of the environment that would tend to fetishise 'nature' against the supposedly deleterious effects of culture.

In 1968, at about the time Long was first developing his practice, Grizedale forester Bill Grant's success in developing a successful sustainable model for the forest as a thriving space for wildlife, for research and for tourism led to him being awarded a Winston Churchill Travelling Fellowship to North America. Though there seemed to be little connection between Grant's activities in the North West, and those of artists such as Long down south, Grant's trip to the United States brought the world of forest management and that of land art together.

He returned with a number of ideas about how to push the development of the forest as an amenity in a number of radical directions. The first and what may seem in retrospect the strangest of these was the Theatre in the Forest. According to his own account, '[A] day time forest experience followed by a cultural experience in the evening fired my imagination'.[5] However, it appeared that this enthusiasm was not widely shared, with any such proposal put before a committee being greeted with 'cries of derision' and numerous objections on the grounds that 'theatres were in towns' and 'how would people get there' and that 'what about the winters', and 'who would finance it?'. Grant did however gain the support of Alex Schouvallof, the director of the North West Arts Association, who, though unable to promise any money, did offer to help with programme suggestions. Thus, after much legal negotiation with the Forestry Commission, who had nothing in their terms of remit to allow for theatres in their properties, and after labouring to convert a hayloft above the coach yard in the grounds of the now demolished Grizedale Hall, the Theatre in the Forest became reality.

With the establishment and successful running of the theatre, Grant and his colleagues could then move onto developing a visual arts programme. This was encouraged by Northern Arts, the regional arts organisation Grizedale had come under, after the reorganisation of county boundaries in 1974. In 1977, the Grizedale Sculpture Trust was formed as part of the Grizedale Society. The main location for sculptures was, in accordance with the tenets of land art, in the open air, along the ten-mile trail, opened in 1973, known as the Silurian Way. This trail, which started at the visitors' centre, was named after geological epoch, a million or so years ago, in which the characteristic grey slate and shale rocks were formed. The first artist to work in Grizedale on the Silurian Way was Richard Harris, who had just graduated from Gloucestershire College of Art and Design, having previously studied at Torquay School of Art.

The ambience of the early work of the Grizedale Sculpture Trust is nicely captured in the book on the Trust published in 1991, *The Grizedale Experience*. It comprises a series of short essays on the development of the Trust, the Theatre and the sculptures, as well as accounts of woodland management in the forest, and the wildlife, the last written by Jack Shard, and a series of photographs of the sculptures themselves, opposite quotations from the artists, describing the work shown or the conditions of its making. These quotations are good indications of the spirit in which the works were made. For example, opposite the first image in the series, that of David Nash's *Running Table* of 1979, there is the following quote from Nash.

We started in February deliberately so we would be there coming out of the winter into Spring, the days becoming progressively longer and warmer.

The trees came into leaf, first the larch, then the willow and and [sic] hazels and the oaks last. I was gently drawn into the metabolism, pace and energy of the forest.[6]

In a recent unpublished interview conducted by Grizedale Arts with Richard Harris, he presents a rather harsher picture of how life was for the first artists in the forest.

It was quite hard actually for the first 3 months... leading up to January. The weather was quite difficult. I was in the forest, very very wet, and I got cold as well, and there was snow.

Harris also describes the first form of accommodation for artists, a caravan. Despite these vicissitudes, artists such as Harris and Nash worked hard to take advantage of the possibilities. The quotation above from the book captures the gentle romanticism of much of the work, which is largely concerned with responding to the natural environment, as opposed to any engagement with broader cultural or political issues. David Kemp's comment on his 1981 work *Scale Green Birdman – or a Departure Lounge* is also apposite.

The Birdman's Hut is a future relic. The birdman has flown away. The remains of his erstwhile magic. In the future's future, we are confronted with the remainders of post-technological shamanism. Birds now inhabit the hut. Nature gently takes over the old place of power. They blend together as the seasons go by and will, sometime, be one again.[7]

Something of the same desire to return to 'nature' is found in Nigel Lloyd's words, opposite the image of his sculpture from 1983, *Stone Red Wallow*.

I felt as though all my senses were becoming much more attuned to the forest environment, working outside every day one became accustomed for seeing and hearing things which I am sure most walkers passing through wouldn't notice. My sense of hearing 'opened' out, the squeaks and screech of birds and buzzards wheeling on the thermals overhead never ceased to amaze me. This 'opening out' of my senses also affected my work. I hope it became more subtle, less brash, more in keeping with the forest.[8]

The Ancient Forester by David Kemp, from 1988, which is, unfortunately perhaps, still extant, is described by its maker as 'a figure of great antiquity' which 'lurks deep in the Gothic forests and wilderness between our ears'. He compares it to Cernunnos, the 'horned Celtic deity' and to Tolkien's Tom Bombadil, as an 'idealised image of man the hunter, the mystic, the guardian', living 'in responsible husbandry with nature', seeking 'a symbiotic relationship with his environment and its renewable resources'. Kemp continues: '[C]entrally-heated, carpeted, cocooned and double-glazed, we are becoming separate from our real life-support systems. Dazzled by the power of our clever machines, we are sawing off the branch we sit on'.[9]

What these quotations have in common, in particular the latter, is the degree to which the works made possible by the Grizedale Sculpture Trust embodied both a particular aesthetic, and indeed ethos, and also a specific, somewhat idealising, attitude towards the environment. They are the authentic voice of English Tolkieno-Heideggerian anti-technological, anti-modernist, romanticism. There is a semi-pantheistic nature mysticism at play in the work and in the responses it engendered. What is particularly interesting is how this mystical reverence towards nature, which must have seemed timeless when the Sculpture Trust first started, now appears as very dated. This is of course not to suggest that the sculptures will never be reevaluated and what they aimed for seen to be worthy, but at the moment of writing at least, they come across as naïve and redolent of a simplistic world-view, in which 'nature' is elevated above a supposedly corrupt and corrupting culture. To some extent the sculptures in the forest, for all that they appear to be engaging with the environment, are still sequestered in a kind of metaphorical white cube, in which the political and cultural complexities of making art, of this or any other sort, are disavowed. In a sense the Trust followed Ruskin's love of nature, but refused his broader political understanding. In an interview with *artcornwall* Adam Sutherland, who would take over directorship of the Trust in 1999, suggests that the development of the Trust was

In terms of art at the time... a long overdue moment, in fact it was in some ways too late. Thatcher was on the point of becoming prime minister, punk was culturally ushering in a new age and politically, culturally, things were mid-change. The work had the connotations of the early 70s and hippie era, but it was also among the first in a new approach to placing art outside of the gallery context, a forerunner of the public art movement.[10]

He goes on to point out that even as the original blueprint of work at the Trust was peaking with Andy Goldsworthy in the mid to late eighties, Damien Hirst was preparing to mount 'Freeze'.

It is perhaps worth noting that the moment of the formation of the Grizedale Sculpture Trust in 1977 was also the year Punk Rock emerged into full public visibility, not least through the publicity engendered by The Sex Pistols' single 'God Save the Queen'. Punk was, in part at least, a reaction against the perceived self-indulgence of 1970s popular culture, in particular the aftermath of the 1960s counterculture, such as hippies and prog rock. Punk, much as it contained its own forms of romanticism, at least involved singing about something resembling the world most people experienced, rather than Robert Plant's invocation of Gollum the evil one, or Yes' endless tales from topographic oceans. The sculptures in the forest seemed, to a great extent, to be part of the same counterculture, taking their cue from Tolkien rather than from the mundane experience of most people at the time, whether in the country or the city. Perhaps such a disavowal of everyday life was understandable at the time. As Dave Haslam points out in his book *Not Abba*, against current nostalgia for an imaginary 1970s of space hoppers, flares and glam rock, it was an extremely grim time, economically, socially and politically.[11]

The visual arts were also beginning to feel the need for a more radical and engaged sensibility that took account of the actual conditions of people's existence, rather than retreating to Tom Bombadil's forest. In 1976, the Institute for Contemporary Arts in London held the final exhibition of the performance art group COUM Transmissions before it reconstituted itself as the experimental rock group Throbbing Gristle. The exhibition, entitled Prostitution, achieved considerable notoriety as a result of its contents, which included not just punk music, but pornographic images of COUM member Cosey Fanni Tutti, and used sanitary towels. The controversial Conservative MP Sir Nicholas Fairbairn responded that the exhibition was a 'sickening outrage. Obscene. Evil. Public money is being wasted here to destroy the morality of our society. These people are the wreckers of civilization!'.[12] At the same time the ICA had also caused controversy with Mary Kelly's exhibition *Post-Partum Document* concerning the mother-child relationship, which featured used nappy liners.

These exhibitions might be seen as part of more general radicalisation of British art that started in the 1970s and continued into the 1980s. The art historian John A. Walker gives an excellent account of this moment in his book *Left Shift: Radical Art in 1970s Britain.*[13] It would be nearly a decade and a half before the Grizedale Sculpture Trust had its punk moment. By the time it did, the British art world had been largely transformed by a generation of punk-influenced artists, known collectively as the Young British Artists or YBAs. The YBAs may now be at the heart of the art world, and to be producing problematic works such as Damien Hirst's *For the Love of God*, described earlier, but in the 1980s they did represent an exciting prospect of art as irreverent and cheeky. The irreverence and iconoclasm of these artists, along with their engagement with popular culture, would eventually penetrate the deep north.

Water Yeat

Water Yeat is a small village near Coniston. Early on in our time in the North, we were invited to a ceilidh in the village hall there, to celebrate the gift of a tea urn and kettle. However, these were not a normal kettle and urn. They were made by the artist Jeremy Deller, working in collaboration with Grizedale Arts in the English Lake District. Deller commissioned John Dillon, a specialist in doing custom paint jobs for Harley Davidson motorcycles and hot rod cars, to decorate a pair of tea urns and teapots. Influenced by American West Coast design, and Latino culture, Dillon had covered the urn and pot with sinuous, flame-like patterns. One of the pair was given to Water Yeat, for use in their village hall, and the other was sold to Tate at the Frieze Art Fair. That version came with the instruction that it was 'not meant to be used'. By contrast, the version given to Water Yeat was intended to be used much as a normal set of such items would be in a village hall (though the village was also free to raise funds by charging for them to be lent to exhibitions).

Though 'Souped Up Urn', as the work was known, was technically by Kane and Deller it also exemplifies the approach of Grizedale Arts, the organisation that made it possible, and indeed offers, in miniature, a perfect example of its unique combination of humour, community engagement and critique of the shibboleths of contemporary art, all in the context of a rural environment far from the metropolitan centres of the art world. This can be seen in the use of a supposedly culturally inferior form of craft, that of customised paint jobs, applied to the most banal of objects, producing a mixture of the ordinary and the kitsch. It is also evident in the gesture of making two versions, one of which is elevated to the status of art object, and thus deprived of any use value, while the other, identical in every aspect, retains that value. Above all, it is the insertion of the latter version into the everyday life of a comparatively remote rural community that exemplifies the radical, humorous and also savagely if politely critical work of Grizedale Arts. This is one of a large number of playful projects that Grizedale Arts has been involved with since the end of the last century.

Grizedale Arts was originally the Grizedale Sculpture Trust, founded by Bill Grant in the 1970s, as described in the previous chapter. By the late 1990s, it was no longer as vibrant as it had been. The quality of the art programme was becoming increasingly patchy, and the Theatre in the Forest, though still popular, was running at a huge loss. Grant, then seventy-five, was persuaded to retire, albeit reluctantly, and the search for a new director for the Trust was undertaken. By 1999, three new directors had been appointed, and all had left. Finally, Adam Sutherland, then running art.tm in Scotland, was persuaded to take the post. Art. tm, which was based in Inverness, was originally established as the Highland Printmakers Workshop and Gallery, and relaunched under its new name in 1996 with Sutherland as director. It had a reputation for encouraging the arts in a rural context, and it was the experience of making this happen that Sutherland was able to bring to Grizedale Arts.

Grizedale Arts is based in a farmhouse, recently refurbished to enable residencies, conferences and meetings, and sited in Grizedale Forest, directly above Coniston Water in the Lake District and Brantwood, Ruskin's Lakeland house. Since 1999 it has pursued an uncompromising and often provocative mission to deconstruct both the presumptions underlying much contemporary art, and also the romantic fantasies about the rural environment that still hold sway, especially in the English Lake District. A small example can be found in the naming of the guest rooms used by artists on residencies at Lawson Park, Grizedale Arts' headquarters above Lake Coniston. Each room has been given a name full of bucolic implications, such as Broadwater Farm and Norris Green. To those ignorant of English social history in the last quarter of the twentieth century, such names may suggest placid rural environments. But of course each name is actually that of an inner city location, often connected with social unrest or even breakdown. Broadwater Farm, for example, is the name of the housing estate in Tottenham in north London, which was the site of violent riots in the mid-1980s, which resulted in the brutal killing of a policeman.

Yet, despite these dystopian references, Grizedale Arts remains a strangely utopian project. In 'War of the Worlds', his essay at the end of *Grizedale Arts: From Complexity to Confusion*, critic Robert Eikmeyer compares Grizedale Arts to H. G. Wells' *The War of the Worlds*. He cites Wells' idea for the original book, which came to him while walking with his brother Frank through the peaceful Surrey landscape. 'Suppose some beings from another planet were to drop out of the sky suddenly', he suggested to his brother. Eikmeyer entertains similar thoughts about the 'beautiful landscape of the Lake District'.[1] The millions of tourists who come to the area every year are of course invaders themselves, even if they are seeking the 'authentic' Lake District. But it is Grizedale Arts itself that he describes as the real invaders, 'an invasion of barbarians from the past combined with aliens of the future, disturbing the harmony and shattering the romantic tranquility of the area'.[2] EIkmeyer suggests that the 'elements and the aesthetics of these projects and festivals are well-known from the alternative cultural movements of the late 1960s and 70s – from hippie-culture, psychedelia, the spectacle of rock music and the D.I.Y. practices of punk, trash-culture, actions, happenings and gatherings etc.'[3] But he notes an important difference in Grizedale's version of this culture in 'that this is not meant as an alternative form of life; this is not a separate culture'.[4]

Eikmeyer suggests that Grizedale Arts offers a joyful version of Bakhtin's carnivalesque, which 'creates the possibility for a multitude of perspectives to coexist peacefully and act together for a certain period of time.' Using language that echoes that of Giorgio Agamben, Eikmeyer declares that Grizedale's 'art farm' at Lawson Park is the basis for a new communist utopian project, 'that allows images, languages or people to transcend their status as goods, and become autonomous.'[5]

Upon his appointment, Sutherland undertook a number of actions which made clear that a new sensibility had arrived at Grizedale Arts. These included closing the economically unviable Theatre in the Forest, having renamed it the Theatre in the Visitor Centre, while the Gallery in the Forest became the Gallery in the Car Park. But perhaps the most visible example of his intentions was the commissioning and erection of a massive billboard, twenty feet wide by fifteen feet high, designed by Calum Stirling, to be erected in a glade at Farra Grain, near the village of Satterthwaite. The artist Marcus Coates was then commissioned to produce the first image for the billboard, which was a photograph of himself sitting disconsolately in his bedroom in the bed and breakfast he was staying in, wearing antlers and a deer mask.

It is hard to imagine a more provocative way of showing that the new direction the Trust was going to take was going to be very different to what had gone on before. Unsurprisingly perhaps, a large number of letters of complaint were received by the organisation. One of the later commissions for the billboard, by a group called The People from Off ('off' being a local word for outsiders), Anne Best, Karen Guthrie, Nina Pope and Simon Poulter, showed a would-be rally driver from Cumbria named Dave Shuttleworth and also featured a blurry image of Sutherland. This was vandalised with the word CRAP cut into the side, a question mark above Shuttleworth, and RESIGN over Sutherland's image. Other, often equally provocative, commissions graced the board in its short existence before it was ceremoniously burnt down as part of a collaboration between Grizedale Arts and the village of Satterthwaite to celebrate the Queen's Golden Jubilee in 2002.

The early work of Grizedale Arts under Sutherland is arguably mostly concerned with a kind of provocative profanation
of the sacralised natural landscape of the Lake District. This was
far more than mere provocation for its own sake, but rather a
series of playful interventions designed to expose the complex
social realities behind the fetishised mountains, forests and lakes.
Among the works and actions in the first year, 1999, were Calum
Stirling's Logo Wall, a drystone wall with embedded sports logos,
which created considerable controversy locally. The People from
Off, as well as using the billboard to promote the career of Dave
Shuttleworth, also arranged 'Limo Day', in which locals, including
an estate agent and a Santa Claus, were ferried around the Lake
District in a white stretch limousine rented for the occasion from
Penrith.

The following year, 2000, the project A Different Weekend
aimed to present contemporary art in the manner of a country
show, with a deliberately amateur feel. Artists organised displays
of local crafts and workshops involving making. Mark Wallinger
ran a face painting stall, and The People from Off launched the
Festival of Lying, in which, among other things, Cumbria's top four
liars performed specially commissioned lies. The works that perhaps best demonstrate Grizedale Arts' interest in the hidden or
obscured side of Cumbria were the films by American artist Jordan
Baseman, who became fascinated by the neglected edges of the
area, in particular the so-called Lake District Peninsulas, which
derive little benefit from the tourist industry.

Baseman made three films. The first, *The Sun Always Shines
on the Righteous*, investigated the Demolition Derby races held
in Barrow, one of the poorest towns in Cumbria, focusing in
particular on Grandad, a forty-something mechanic who fixes
the cars before the races, and Adam, an overweight transvestite
comedian, who is part of the pre-race entertainment. Baseman's
second film, *Born to Run*, is about Alan and Chris, proprietors of a
mobile burger van stationed near the race stadium, and engages

with their hopes and dreams. His final Grizedale film, *The One about the Camel*, is constructed out of hours of footage of two men who worked in the Co-op in Ulverston, another poor town in the area, and whose rambling conversation is full of invective against their lives, their jobs and their ex-wives. The title refers to a joke told by one of the men, about a camel considering its fate as a resident in a zoo.

According to the Grizedale Arts' website, plans to show these films in the forest were cancelled by the Forestry Commission at the last moment, due to fears that 'Travellers' would take up residence there, once invited. Baseman's work was arguably crucial to how Grizedale Arts developed in the following years. His videos exposed the complex and far from comfortable social realities of life in the poorer sections of Cumbria, elements which most tourists resolutely ignored in favour of the sublime experience of the hills and of nature. His work can be seen and indeed was seen by some as exploitative and voyeuristic, a kind of condescending pornography of the underclass. Yet it can also be seen as a valuable exercise in understanding communities and individuals who are not easily assimilated into a picturesque vision of rural life.

One of the features of much of Grizedale's work in this period was the deliberate bringing of supposedly underclass, or at least lowbrow, activities into the Lake District. In 2002 for example, the Visitor Centre in the forest was used to host a car boot sale, in which, among more plausible items, copies of major video art works were sold for one pound. Three years later, Karen Guthrie and Nina Pope organised a Lakeland version of *It's a Knockout*, a lowbrow television game show from the 1970s. (The presenter during much of the show's lifetime, Stuart Hall, was recently imprisoned for historic sex offences, some against very young children.) In the original version, contestants wore rubber foam suits to compete in deliberately ludicrous games. In Pope and Guthrie's version, the foam suits were of John Ruskin, Alfred Wainwright, Beatrix Potter and Donald Campbell.

The increasing reputation of Grizedale Arts led to an invitation in 2004 to organise an exhibition at MoMA PS1 in New York, the Museum of Modern Art's space for exhibitions of emerging and adventurous new art. The title of the exhibition was *Romantic Detachment*, and it aimed to examine the romanticisation of one culture by another, in particular the mutual idealisation between the United Kingdom and the United States. It critiqued the standard image of Romantic landscape exemplified by the Lake District and sought to capture an alternative romanticism to that found in high art, as exemplified in the Wild West, in music culture and in folk traditions. The exhibition involved forty artists, many of whom had worked with Grizedale Arts in Cumbria, but also American artists such as William Pope L. The main exhibition space in PS1 was turned into a studio to coordinate live engagements with individuals and groups sited all over New York and elsewhere. The show led to other events, such as *We Are Seven*, in which seven artists from the United States undertook a residency at the Wordsworth Trust in Grasmere.

Romantic Detachment may be considered the apogee of Grizedale Arts' critique of English Romanticism. The year 2005 saw a commission that took the work of Grizedale Arts towards a far closer involvement with local communities. This was also the moment when Alistair Hudson arrived to take up the role of deputy director after a number of earlier incumbents had left. Hudson, who remained at Grizedale for ten years before taking up the post of director of the Middlesborough Institute of Modern Art (MIMA), was central to the shift towards a more community-oriented role for the organisation. He has recently moved from Middlesborough to head both the Whitworth and City Galleries in Manchester, following Maria Balshaw's move to be director of Tate. The organisation had already revived a Victorian event known as the Coniston Water Festival as part of Cumbriana Proof, the project that also saw the Lakeland *It's a Knockout*. In the same year, the Egremont and Area Regeneration Partnership commissioned

the organisation to create a programme of public art projects celebrating local culture for the town of Egremont in West Cumbria.
Like Barrow and Ulverston, the towns featured in Baseman's films,
Egremont is one of the parts of Cumbria that is not greatly visited by
tourists. The only reason it would have impinged on most people's
consciousness recently was as the centre of the search for gunman
Derrick Bird, who shot several people in the area in 2010, two of
them in Egremont itself, before committing suicide. The town's
main employer is Sellafield and the National Nuclear Laboratory.
It does however have a number of notable features, including what
was the deepest iron ore mine in Western Europe, Florence Mine
(which closed in 2008), and a royal charter for a market and fair
that dates back to 1266. The annual fair, known as the Crab Fair,
hosts the World Gurning Championship. 'Gurning' is a dialect term
of disputed origin for making a distorted facial expression, and the
Crab Fair is the most famous competition for gurners.

For the commission, entitled Creative Egremont, Grizedale
Arts worked with a number of artists and people from the local community, to produce various interventions, including renovating
a bus shelter, setting up Egremont FM, a short-term community
radio station, and, with Jeremy Deller and Alan Kane, reinstating
the Egremont Greasy Pole. Such poles, which were made slippery
and difficult to grip, and which contestants attempted to climb,
were a feature of fairs from all over the world, with the Crab Fair
being one of the most famous. A side of mutton was traditionally
placed at the top for the prize. However, safety and insurance con-
siderations had meant the pole climbing was discontinued there
in 2004. Deller and Kane's version is made of carbon fibre and
is a permanent installation, floodlit at night, unlike the previous
poles, which were wooden and temporary, only erected for the
duration of the fair. The other major project of Creative Egremont
has been the exploitation of Florence Mine's iron ore reserves to
create a new paint of a rich russet colour, named Egremont Red,
thus enabling a re-opening of the mine.

Grizedale Arts' increasing involvement with community projects led to an invitation to contribute to the 2006 Echigo-Tsumari Triennale in Japan. This took the form of a month-long residency involving Grizedale Arts' staff members and artists in a remote village named Toge that is near the site of the Triennale, and which sees an influx of visitors during the time it takes place, and has got an ageing population much like the Lake District. The remote terrain in which the village is located is also some-what similar to the Lake District. The artists worked with the villagers on a number of projects, after which villagers and artists performed together at an arts festival in Tokyo. The following year, some of the villagers made the trip to the Lake District, where they helped develop the Lawson Park farm by building rice paddies and ran wild food workshops with local chefs, including Simon Rogan, who runs the Michelin-starred restaurant L'Enclume in Cartmel in the Cumbrian peninsula. Finally, they concluded their visit with a Japanese Country Café in the Coniston Institute in which plants such as bracken, found all over the Lake District, were cooked Japanese style, in tempura – bracken being a deli-cacy in Japan.

As the building of the paddy fields suggests, along with greater community engagement, Grizedale Arts was also increas-ingly involved with agriculture and gardening. Accordingly, one of Grizedale Arts' major projects has been the refurbishment of Lawson Park into its headquarters and site for residencies as well as for the experimental farm and garden activities. As part of Cumbriana Proof, artist Olivia Plender remade some of the costumes worn by the Kibbo Kift Kindred. These were then worn by people in a procession through Coniston, singing Kibbo Kift songs, led by veteran film director and Lakeland resident Ken Russell in white shorts, to Coniston's Old Hall, where there was a lecture by Kibbo Kift expert Harry White. Russell then delivered a lecture on a local cave-dwelling eccentric named Milican Dalton, who claimed to have invented shorts.

Sutherland had leased the farmhouse in 2000, soon after arriving as director, and had started work on the ornamental garden in 2001. His partner, artist and filmmaker Karen Guthrie, joined him in 2002. When Sutherland first moved in, Lawson Park was still arranged as a typical Cumbrian farmhouse with a cottage at one end and a barn at the other. Though it was leased by Sutherland as his own residence rather than on behalf of the organisation, it nevertheless was extensively used as a venue for artistic events, while the gardens were developed as an ongoing project. In 2008, after the signing of a forty-two-year lease between the owner of the building, the Forestry Commission and Grizedale Arts, a year-long project followed to turn Lawson Park into the organisation's headquarters and the location of an experiment in art, ecology and lifestyle, as well as of a collection of British design artefacts from the Arts and Crafts movement to the present day. Costing over a million pounds, raised partly through the sale of Summerhill, a building owned by Grizedale Arts near Hawkshead, and partly through funders such as Northern Rock and the Arts Council, this conversion took over a year.

It was also at this point that Grizedale Arts began to develop projects in the village of Coniston, which sits on the other side of Coniston Water from Lawson Park. Though originally an agricultural and mining village, it became a popular tourist site in the nineteenth century owing to the building of a branch of the Furness Railway to a station in the village, and also because of Ruskin, whose house, Brantwood, is on the other side of the Water. Ruskin's presence is still much in evidence, given that he is buried in the local churchyard, under an ornate Arts and Crafts cross, decorated with, among other things, a swastika, and also because of the local Mechanics' Institute, which he helped to renovate and rebuild some twenty years after its founding in the mid-nineteenth century. Among the amenities offered by the refurbished Institute were a library, a theatre, artists' studios, a bathhouse, a kitchen and various minerals, fossils, antiquities and paintings donated by Ruskin and Collingwood. In short, it offered what was deemed necessary for a complete education for the working man or woman in Coniston. After Ruskin's death, the Ruskin Museum was founded in his honour, and was built in 1911. In the last few years, Grizedale has worked with the Institute and the Ruskin Museum to revive the original intentions of the Institute as conceived by Ruskin.

There are many arts organisations offering new forms of engaged and politically motivated art practice, such as Platform, Woodbine 1882 and The Dark Mountain Project, but they share a kind of earnestness entirely lacking in Grizedale. Perhaps we need a different kind of discourse with which to think about what Grizedale is doing, which is not history of art, or art theory, or even cultural theory. Maybe it is something more like speculative fiction, or, in the light of recent developments within philosophy, speculative realist fiction. The recently emergent philosophical movement Speculative Realism owes much to the pulp science or horror fiction of H. P. Lovecraft, and some of those connected with it attempt their own forms of fiction as a means of philosophical adventuring inspired by Lovecraft's strange visions.

Standing in Grizedale Forest, on the paddy fields at the back of Lawson Park on a cold afternoon in late November, it is easy to believe that civilisation has collapsed and that Grizedale Arts is a pocket of resistance to encroaching barbarism in a kind of cultural survivalism. It is reminiscent for example of Sarah Hall's novel *The Carhullen Army*, which is actually set in a post-catastrophe northern Lake District, or Marlen Haushofer's novel *Die Wand* (*The Wall*), in which a woman staying in a hunting lodge in the Austrian mountains finds that she appears to be the last human survivor of a catastrophe and that she cannot leave the area owing to the presence of an invisible wall.[6] The book recounts her attempts to survive in this situation, without any of the amenities of civilisation. What is particularly strange is that, on the other side of the wall, time seems to have stopped.

Happy Mount Park

The seaside resort of Morecambe runs northwards from the mouth of the River Lune. Once prosperous, it is now sad and down-at-heel, lacking even the vulgar exuberance of its Lancashire rival Blackpool. The sea itself is intensely disappointing, shallow and silty at best, and often simply not there. The tides in the Bay of Morecambe go out for miles, and the sands that are revealed are treacherous and even fatal. The town has some interesting buildings and a certain derelict charm. The rock-bottom house prices however suggest that it is not prospering. I like Morecambe, but most visitors to this part of world tend to bypass it and go to the Lakes.

There are, however, some sights worth seeing in Morecambe. One is the Midland Hotel, an art deco masterpiece designed by Oliver Hill and built in 1933. It originally contained specially commissioned works by Eric Gill and Eric Ravilious, though only Gill's works remain: a beautiful relief behind the reception desk, showing Odysseus welcomed from the Sea by Nausicaa; a carved map of the North West of England in the room next door; a medallion of Neptune and Triton on the ceiling above the stairwell; and two carved seahorses set high up above the entrance. The Ravilious mural in the Rotunda Bar was destroyed, though a homage to it is now in its place. The Midland was pretty much derelict by the beginning of the century, but has since been restored to something close to its original condition.

Another sight in Morecambe to be recommended is one that is highly evocative for people of my generation, those born in the early 1960s. Along the front, north of the Midland, there is a statue of Eric Morecambe, the comedian, who was born there. His real name was Eric Bartholomew, and he adopted Morecambe as his stage name, presumably as a tribute to his town of birth. The statue shows him in the pose familiar from the dance he and Ernie Wise did during the closing credits of their show, to the sound of the song 'Bring Me Sunshine'.

Morecambe also has the world's most entropic second-hand bookshop, further up the front, which is something like a Kurt Schwitters' *Merzbau*, in which every space is filled with shelves of books, with traces of order, presumably a legacy of an earlier time of greater attention to such matters, and a considerable degree of disorder. There is also Happy Mount Park, which features a pirate-themed playground, a café, a 'splash park', adventure golf, a miniature railway and other such amenities. I once went there hoping to find the traces of one of the North West's most notorious sites of failure, Crinkley Bottom, a theme park devoted to the Mr Blobby character from the television programme *Noel's House Party*. The host of the show, Noel Edmonds, is one of those TV personalities whose success and appeal is somewhat opaque. Mr Blobby is similarly confusing; a charmless round, pink and yellow-spotted, vaguely human-shaped creature, 'his' only utterance being 'blobby blobby blobby' in electronically distorted tones. Mr Blobby had the UK Christmas no. 1 single in 1993 with a song entitled 'Mr Blobby'. In the *New York Times* Elizabeth Kolbert compared Mr Blobby to Barney, the popular purple dinosaur on American children's television, though Barney is much more benign than Blobby. Kolbert quotes the creator of Blobby, Mike Leggo, about his appeal as 'a product of his essential innocence'. He 'really wears his heart on his sleeve'. But, continues Kolbert,

watching Mr. Blobby at work, his green plastic eyes spinning maniacally, one has to wonder whether his appeal to this nation of Shakespeare, Milton and Philip Larkin isn't a bit more complex. His frozen smile has a malevolent curve. Blobby is Barney without his medication.[1]

She goes on to quote a story from *The Sun* in which 'Mr. Blobby reduced a little girl to tears when he threw her birthday cake to the floor during a show in Luton, near London.'

Despite his lack of appeal, Edmonds possesses a kind of genius. One example of this, in *Noel's House Party*, was the greatest piece of television I ever witnessed. The programme went out live and Edmonds took full advantage of this to pull off an astonishing *coup de théatre*. A camera was hidden in the home in which the show was regularly watched (presumably with the connivance of someone in the household), facing the place where the viewer or viewers sat. Suddenly the unsuspecting viewer found themselves watching themselves, watching themselves on television. For some reason I caught this moment without any knowledge of what was about to happen. It was the best piece of performance art I had ever seen, and still is. For a moment the viewer in question had a look of absolute confusion, having been confronted by something that was radically incomprehensible, a kind of rip in the space–time continuum, in which the television universe turned in on itself. I doubt Philip K. Dick or William Burroughs could have imagined anything more dislocating. The other piece of evidence for Edmonds' genius is Mr Blobby his- (or maybe its-) self. As commentators mentioned above realised, he or it was far from the benign comedy figure he was presented as. He is far more complex and strange.

This may be the reason the show was so incredibly popular. On the back of this success Edmonds had opened a Blobby theme park in Cricket St Thomas, Somerset, in 1994. It was initially very successful, which persuaded the Morecambe Town Council to open a similar theme park in Happy Mount Park. Only one councillor opposed the plan. The council hoped to attract a quarter of a million visitors to Morecambe, which was then, as now, desperately in need of regeneration. The opposing councillor, Shirley Burns, said that 'there was no way people were going to queue to see a few small houses and a man in a Mr Blobby suit, they would only go if Noel Edmonds himself was going to be there every day. I really believe that people got carried away with the whole thing.'[2] Ignoring Burns' doubts, the council signed a three-year contract with Edmonds' Unique Group, and the park opened at the end of July 1994. The venture failed to reach its financial targets, and was closed down following a council vote in November of the same year. To add to the fiasco, predictably becoming known as Blobbygate, Unique Group sued the council for defamation, and won damages of nearly a million pounds. The whole affair cost local taxpayers over two and a half million pounds. I hoped to find some remains of Crinkley Bottom in Happy Mount Park; perhaps the last vestiges of Mr Blobby's time there, maybe a pink and yellow toilet from Dunblobbin, his house. However, as far as I can tell, there is nothing left of the fiasco that was Crinkley Bottom.

From Happy Mount Park, as from anywhere on Morecambe's front, one looks across the Bay straight over to the mountains of the Lake District. This view has always been one of Morecambe's main attractions. It also highlights the incongruent juxtaposition of the 'unspoilt', sublime and paradisiacal beauty of the Lakes and the rundown vulgarity of Morecambe, exemplified by the brief presence of Crinkley Bottom there. What could be less alike than the romantic vision of mountains and lakes found in Wordsworth and a man in a pink and yellow-spotted suit going 'blobby blobby blobby'. Yet a proper non-dual ecological consciousness would embrace both equally as part of our environment, equally precious, equally valuable.

At some level, Mr Blobby is one of the most uncannily uncomfortable creations I have encountered. Even the name is brilliantly unsettling, working as it does in the tension between the apparent normality and formality of identity, signified by the title 'Mr', with all its suggestions of propriety, autonomy, completeness, subjectivity, individuality, and the name itself, with its implications of formlessness, of something without proper shape, something that is not really a thing at all. One of the best expressions of the fear blobbiness invokes is the 1958 film *The Blob*. A classic B-movie, translating Cold War nuclear paranoia into science fiction, it features an alien amoeboid entity that lands on earth and consumes and dissolves communities and buildings, growing to monstrous proportions as it does. It has a parallel in the non-fictional universe. *Pylarum Polycephalum* is a slime mould consisting of a single cell. It has many 'heads' as its Latin name suggests, but no brain. Nevertheless, it can, apparently, learn and even communicate what it has learnt to other slime moulds with which it amalgamates. Some scientists call it 'the blob'. The word 'blob', as Edmonds surely realised, connotes something deeply unsettling, especially in relation to the human, for boundaries, borders and limits. That Mr Blobby's speech is limited to the word 'blobby' is an almost avant-garde deconstruction of language as composed of meaningful limits.

George Bataille's infamous definition of *l'informe*, 'formless', describes the universe as nothing more than a blob of spittle. For Bataille the universe as a gob or blob of spit is closely allied to a crushed insect, a spider or an earthworm.[3] ('Researching' this chapter on Google, I discover that there is a form of sexual fetishism devoted to the crushing of insects. Its exponents are known as 'crush freaks'.) The image of a crushed insect is central to the extraordinary book *The Passion According to G. H.*, the novel by the Brazilian writer Clarice Lispector. It is nearly impossible to describe, let alone do justice, to this work. It tells the story of the eponymous G. H. a well-to-do sculptress from Rio de Janeiro, who enters the room recently and abruptly vacated by her maid, about whom she knows little or nothing. Expecting a mess, she finds the room bare, except for a mysterious drawing on the wall, of a man, a woman and a dog, which she interprets as a sign of the maid's hostility towards her. She decides to clean the cupboard and becomes utterly transfixed by a cockroach, which she has crushed in the cupboard door, and, though still living, is exuding a white paste or pus. The cockroach is, at first, an unwelcome reminder of the

poverty of her childhood. Over the course of the narrative, if that's
the right word, G. H. realises that she must overcome her disgust at
the roach and what oozes out of it, and actually eat it.

sitting there and unmoving, I still had not stopped looking with great disgust, yes, still with disgust at the yellowed white paste atop the roach's
grayness. And I knew that as long as I was disgusted, the world would
elude me and I would elude me. I knew that the basic error in living was
being disgusted by a roach. Being disgusted by kissing the leper was my
erring the first life within me – since being disgusted contradicts me,
contradicts my matter within me.[4]

When G. H. eventually manages to put the cockroach in her
mouth, what she calls 'the tiniest act', she experiences a kind of
mystical or religious epiphany that takes her beyond anything
human or that can be expressed in language, in a non-human
apprehension of the divine redolent of the pantheism of Spinoza.

Finally, finally, my casing had really broken and without limit I was.
Through not being, I was. To the ends of whatever I was not, I was.
Whatever I am not, I am. All shall be within me, if I shall not be; for 'I' is
just one of the instantaneous spasms of the world. My life does not have
a merely human meaning, it is so much greater – so much greater that,
as humanity goes, it makes no sense. Of the general organization that as
greater than I, I had previously only perceived the fragments. But now,
I was much less than human – and I would only fulfill my specifically
human destiny, as I was handing myself over, to whatever was no longer I,
to what is already inhuman.[5]

The cockroach is the epitome of abject animality, almost
always treated with absolute disgust. Even the most environmen-
tally sensitive individual probably does not care that much either
for or about cockroaches. I am sure advocates of rewilding would
baulk a bit if their new wilderness meant cockroaches rather than,
say, wolves. In the context of Auschwitz this disgust takes on a

more ominous meaning; one of the ways in which the horror of the Shoah was made possible was to regard Jews as not human, and precisely as vermin such as insects, cockroaches. As Shoah survivor Sol Einhorn puts it, 'the Jew to the German was a cockroach... if you step on a cockroach... it doesn't mean anything. The same thing, exactly the same thing, the Jew was to a German – a cockroach.'[6]

This idea of the Jew as a verminous insect was taken more or less literally by the Nazis. After the First World War, when the Germans were forbidden to continue to gas warfare research, the laboratories where such research had taken place developed a number of variants of hydrogen cyanide gas for use as an insecticide. One such product was named Zyklon A. Another company, Tesch and Stabenow, further developed this to produce its version, known as Zyklon B.

In 1945, three hundred Jewish children, all of whom had been orphaned as a result of the Holocaust, or, rather, the Shoah, arrived at the Calgarth Estate between Windermere and Ambleside in the heart of the Lake District, to be housed there temporarily. Having been in the Theresienstadt concentration camp, they were taken to Prague, and from there flown to Carlisle, and then to their final destination in the Lakes. The library in Windermere houses a permanent exhibition about the 'boys', as they were known, entitled 'From Auschwitz to Ambleside'.

One of the consistent tropes in the exhibition literature and in the video interviews with the boys is the idea that these children went from hell to heaven, or paradise. One of the 'boys', David Hirszfeld, testified that 'it felt like heaven'. Mayer Hersh suggested that 'it was like coming to heaven because we came from hell'. For Jack Aizenberg, 'We came from hell to paradise'. So insistent is the idea of their destination as paradise or heaven that the journey from Theresienstadt to Calgarth has become known as the 'Paradise Route'.

This narrative of redemption through nature of the most catastrophic barbarity of all time makes me uncomfortable. The

words of Adorno come to mind, that it is barbaric to write poetry
after Auschwitz,[7] and perhaps it is also barbaric to seek solace or
healing in a place like the Lake District after Auschwitz as well,
and perhaps to write about 'nature' more generally. For me it is
hard to imagine how we can continue to enjoy the Romantic ethos
of the Lake District after the brute fact of Auschwitz. All that it is
supposed to represent for us seems now impossible; redemption
through nature; a sense of the world's fundamental benignity; an
experience of the immanence of the Divine. Literary critic Geoffrey
Hartman, whose early work was on Wordsworth, but later turned
to questions of the Holocaust and witnessing, expressed a similar
thought. He describes a scene he had witnessed in New England
in mid-October. It is a lyrical description of the gold, falling leaves
of the many maples, and of children playing among piles of raked
leaves. He then moves to a different register.

I am on my way to give a lecture on the Holocaust, when I come across
the pastoral scene. What am I doing here, I ask myself. How can I talk
about such matters, here. I cannot reconcile scenes like this with others
I know about.

In a fleeting montage I see or dream I see the green cursed fields at
Auschwitz. A cold calm has settled on them. The blood does not cry from
the ground. Yet no place, no wood, meadow, sylvan scene will now be
the same.[8]

In 1937, even before the full horror of the death camps had
started, Lucy Dawidowicz, a graduate student in English at
Columbia University, asked herself a rhetorical question: 'What
did Wordsworth matter to me at such a time?'.

There is an irony here given that the Holocaust itself was, for
Hitler, an attempt to restore a paradisiacal condition. As Yale historian Timothy Snyder puts it in his book *Black Earth*, 'When paradise falls and humans are separated from nature, a character who
is neither human or natural, such as the serpent of Genesis, takes

the blame' and corrupts the species. According to Snyder, Hitler believed that 'the bringer of knowledge of good and evil on the earth, the destroyer of Eden, was the Jew', by telling humans that they were 'above other animals, and that they had the capacity to decide their future for themselves', and by introducing the 'false distinction between politics and nature, between humanity and struggle'. Thus Hitler saw his destiny, to redeem 'the original sin of Jewish spirituality and restore the paradise of blood'.[9]

The question of Auschwitz is more than a historical catastrophe or disaster. It also radically brings into question meaning and language itself, as well as subjectivity, experience and witnessing. What Auschwitz makes impossible, suggests Maurice Blanchot, is any Romantic, Wordsworthian presumption about the ability of language to heal the split between nature and culture through poetry. Blanchot refers to it as the 'holocaust, the absolute event of history – which is a date in history – that utter-burn where all history took fire, where the movement of Meaning was swallowed up'.[10]

Clearly, the idea of the cockroach as a figure of the alien other we wish to destroy animates Muriel Rukeyser's poem 'St Roach', in which, addressing the eponymous roach, she claims that 'For that I never knew you, I only learned to dread you/for that I never touched you, they told me you are filth'. Rukeyser goes on by describing seeing 'my people making war on you... crushing you, stamping you to death, they poured boiling/water on you, they flushed you down'. She laments that she did not know the roach's poems or sayings, and cannot speak its language or sing its songs: 'But that we say you are filthing our food/But that we know you not at all'. However, she notices this particular insect, 'lighter than the other in color', which she reaches down and touches.

Today I touched one of you for the first time.
You were startled, you ran, you fled away
Fast as a dancer, light, strange and lovely to the touch.
I reach, I touch, I begin to know you.[11]

Rukeyser still anthropomorphises the cockroach, as if it could be reduced to a human meaning. If the roach was capable of sophisticated sentience (and who is to say it is not) it would probably regard such an approach with considerable contempt. This is the mistake that Lispector's G. H. makes at first, comparing the cockroach, comparing it to 'a bride in black jewels',[12] thus translating it into human terms, and, in the words of Benjamin Moser, she thus 'grotesquely personifies' it. She must learn to encounter it as it is and as profoundly inhuman, the 'ultimate inhumanity', without 'human hope and beauty'.[13]

What I had always found repulsive in roaches is that they were obsolete yet still present. Knowing that they were already on the Earth, and the same as they are today, even before the first dinosaurs appeared, knowing that the first man already found them proliferated and crawling alive, knowing that they had witnessed the formation of the great deposits of oil and coal in the world, and there they were during the great advance and then during the great retreat of the glaciers – the peaceful resistance. I knew that roaches could resist for more than a month without food or water. And that they could even make a useable nutritive substance from wood. And that, even after being crushed, they slowly decompressed and kept on walking. Even when frozen, they kept on marching once thawed.[14]

According to Lispector's biographer Benjamin Moser, she is the writer 'who answers the question that Adorno poses that he later took back, that there can be no poetry after Auschwitz. She's the one that answers that question, and she answers it in a positive way'. According to Moser, facing 'the white goo which oozes from the roach's body G. H. realizes that she, too, is a random eruption, like an animal, or a rock, and in recognition of this realization, brings the goo to her lips and tastes of it'. For Moser, this is what is left when God is no longer approachable. 'What's left is this vocation for the divine and the state of grace and this desire to discover inside oneself the breath of life. And that's the roach. She approaches God with disgust and with fear and trembling, not philosophically but really in her guts.' Moser suggests this is a post-Auschwitz theology. 'She is staring Auschwitz in the face her whole life.'[15]

Compared to the cockroach, the existence of humans is both an extraordinarily recent phenomenon but also one that is likely to be brief. The cockroach is among the oldest species on earth, possibly emerging 350 million years ago, putting homo sapien's mere 200,000 years of existence into context. Proverbially it is supposed to be the one species that would survive a nuclear holocaust (though this turns out to be, in strictly scientific terms, untrue).

Lispector is sometimes described as the 'Brazilian Kafka', and her cockroach does bring to mind the monstrous insect which Gregor Samsa becomes in *The Metamorphosis* (which may or may not be a cockroach. Vladimir Nabokov was certain Kafka intended it to be a beetle). Kafka's stories are, of course, open to endless interpretation. One interpretation might be that Samsa's transformation is a figure for what comes after the human. Rosi Braidotti, however, describes Lispector as the anti-Kafka, particularly in relation to *The Passion According to G. H.* Braidotti sees this text as evincing a concern with gender and the feminine, entirely absent from Kafka's own entomological narrative. She argues this in the context of a discussion of what she calls 'Becoming Insect'.[16] For Braidotti, 'insect life dwells between different states of in-between-ness, arousing the same spasmodic reactions in humans as the monstrous, the sacred, the alien'. Insects 'exacerbate the human power of understanding to the point of implosion'. In 'the post-nuclear historical context, they have become the sign of a widespread repertoire of angst-ridden fears and deep anxiety'.[17] Similarly, for Steve Shaviro 'insect life is an alien presence we can neither assimilate nor expel'.[18] Shaviro sees insects as far more advanced than humans in their capacity to change radically and routinely in their own lives. By contrast, humans are so bound up with memory, history, education and tradition, through which we are oppressed by the dead weight of the past.[19] Insects can adapt to changed environmental circumstances far faster than we can.

But we are much more insect than we usually know. We are made up of alien life, in the form of microbes, bacteria, viruses. Even language can be thought of, *à la* William Burroughs, as a kind of virus. The human fantasy of proper autonomy, completeness and identity, as well as that of self-conscious interiority, are delusions. As Barbara Ehrenreich points out, our bodies, far from being coherent organisations of cells, microbes and myriad other components, are hotch-potch accumulations of material. We 'contain multitudes' as the title of a recent book on our bodies has it, but this Whitmanesque sentiment conceals the fact that we are, in fact, warring agglomerations of antagonistic elements. Shaviro therefore suggests that we should cultivate our inner housefly or cockroach rather than our inner child, and let 'selectional processes do their work of hatching alien eggs' in our bodies. Even if we can kill individual insects, we cannot 'extricate ourselves from the *insect continuum* that marks life on this planet'.[20] The same selectional forces that change insect bodies are also at work in our own bodies and brains, shaping our neurons and even our thoughts. Thus, for Shaviro, we must reject all distinctions of inside and outside, nature and culture, genetics and environment, biology and sociology. He finds inspiration for this in entomology as being far more open to difference and change, and more attentive to the body, without delusional fantasies of redemption and transcendence found in Marxism and psychoanalysis.[21] What Shaviro calls the 'bizarre, irreversible contingencies of natural history and cultural history alike' resist all attempts to give life meaning, a goal or permanence. Shaviro quotes Maurice Maeterlinck: 'The insect brings with him something that does not seem to belong to the customs, the moral, the psychology of our globe. One could say that it comes from another planet, more monstrous, more dynamic, more insensate, more atrocious, more infernal than ours', and then adds that 'such alien splendor is precisely what defines the cruelty and beauty of our world'.[22]

Conclusion

In the spring when I was finishing this book, my wife and I went for a walk in the Yorkshire Dales. We had found a description of a little-known round near Sedbergh, where we were unlikely to encounter too many other walkers. Quite a way into the valley in which we were walking we came across a ruined and deserted farmhouse, probably Georgian or early Victorian, with a number of outbuildings, all made of the local grey stone. The roof had fallen in, as could be seen through the holes in the ground-floor ceiling. It looked as if it had been last occupied a couple of decades ago, if not longer, and the surrounding environment was in the process of reclaiming the house, with weeds pushing through any space they could find. Such a building is as much of the environment, the local ecology, as any tree or river, and makes the landscape what it is as much as they do. The combination of proliferating plant life, the ongoing collapse of the building's structure, and its eeriness reminded me (as such places always do) of the 'Zone' in Andrei Tarkovsky's film *Stalker*.

The 'Zone' is an area which has received some kind of alien visitation, and there are a large number of alien artefacts still there much like the detritus of a roadside picnic (the name of the novel on which the film is based). There is nothing 'natural' in the usual sense about this space, and certainly nothing pastoral and consolatory about it. Indeed, it is dangerous enough to be tightly guarded by the military, despite which the eponymous stalker, a kind of Dostoyevskian Christ figure, can take those who wish into the Zone. The Zone is not beautiful in the conventional sense, and yet, through Tarkovsky's extraordinary visual attention it is utterly compelling and completely other.

As a number of commentators have pointed out, the Zone in *Stalker* eerily anticipates the 'Zone of Alienation' which contains Chernobyl. Adding to the similarities, Stalker was filmed partly in a disused hydro plant in Estonia, which was downstream from a chemical plant that was emitting toxic substances into the river. Tarkovsky and a number of other people involved in the filming subsequently contracted and died of cancer of the bronchial tube. Yet the presumption that the Chernobyl explosion was an unmitigated disaster, or as dangerous as people assumed it would be, has been questioned. The number of deaths and incidents of cancer that can be directly attributed to the event is also disputed, while the effects of radiation on the animal population have been remarkably slight. Most peculiar of all is the news that, having been largely abandoned by humans, it has become an unofficial nature reserve, with rare species proliferating. This is not to underestimate the dangers of nuclear power, but rather to testify to the extraordinary resilience and responsiveness of the environment, and also to its utter contingency.

Though entering the Zone takes him away from his family and puts him into great danger, the stalker clearly finds something deeply wonderful about being there. In his book on *Stalker*, Geoff Dyer describes the moment when the visitors enter the Zone.

It is every bit as lovely as Stalker claims – and at the same time quite ordinary. The air is full of the sound of birds, of wind in the trees, running water. Mist, muted greens. Weeds and plants swaying in the breeze. The tangled wires of a tilted telegraph pole. The rusting remains of a car. We are in another world that is no more than this world perceived with unprecedented attentiveness.[1]

In one of the most extraordinary scenes in the film, having just arrived in the Zone with his guests, he breaks away and rolls ecstatically in long, wild grass. This is a profoundly erotic gesture inasmuch as it is clearly an act of love. Dyer points out that landscapes such as these had been seen before, but 'their beingness had not been seen in this way'. 'Tarkovsky reconfigured the world, brought this landscape – this way of seeing the world – into existence'.[2] Dyer describes how, after Stalker proclaims 'home at last' on entering the Zone, 'the whole landscape seems to be emerging from sleep, rubbing the mist from its eyes, as if it had been stirred into consciousness by the fact of being seen, appreciated, visited, needed. We have only just arrived and already there is a sense, dormant and untapped, of slumbering sentience about the place'. For Dyer, this is what certain artists are capable of doing, 'to make the rest of us see what has always been there', and cites the photographer Walker Evans as opening our eyes, not just to the 'unchanging, eternal, natural world' but also to 'the sagging shacks, wrecked cars and fading signs of America in the thirties'.[3]

Notes

Introduction

1 Agamben, George. *The Idea of Prose*. State University of New York Press, 1995, 63–4.
2 Davidson, Peter. *The Idea of North*. Reaktion Books, 2005.
3 Riley, Bronwen. *The Edge of the Empire: A Journey to Britannia: From the Heart of Rome to Hadrian's Wall*. Head of Zeus, 2015.
4 Wordsworth, William. *Poetical Works* eds. Thomas Hutchinson and Ernest de Sélincourt, vol. 5. Oxford University Press, 1936, 313.
5 Ibid., vol. 2, 216.
6 Kinsella, John. *Polysituatedness: A Poetics of Displacement*. Oxford University Press, 2017, 15.
7 Clark, Nigel. *Inhuman Nature: Sociable Living on a Dynamic Planet*. SAGE Publications, 2011, xii.
8 Ibid., xiii.
9 Wordsworth, William, Jonathan Wordsworth, M. H. Abrams, and Stephen Gill. *The Prelude, 1799, 1805, 1850: Authoritative Texts, Context and Reception, Recent Critical Essays*. W. W. Norton & Company, 1979, 483.
10 Ibid., 50.
11 MacFarlane, Robert. 'How Nan Shepherd Remade My Vision of the Cairngorms', *The Guardian*, 27 December 2013.
12 Thacker, Eugene. *In the Dust of This Planet*. Zero Books, 2011, 1.
13 Ibid., 3.
14 Ibid., 5–6.
15 Jameson, Fredric. *Archaeologies of the Future: The Desire Called Utopia and Other Science Fictions*. Verso, 2005, 107f.
16 Ibid., 111.
17 John, Emma. 'Richard Powers: We're Completely Alienated from Everything Else Alive', *The Guardian*, 16 June 2018.
18 Price, Lucien. *Dialogues of Alfred North Whitehead*. David R Godine, 2001, 209.
19 Ehrenreich, Barbara. *Natural Causes: Life, Death and the Illusion of Control*. Granta Books, 2018, 202–3.
20 McLellan, John. 'NONDUAL ECOLOGY: In Praise of Wildness and In Search of Harmony With Everything That Moves'. www.colorado.edu/econ/courses/roper/sustainable-economics/nondual-ecology/nondual-ecology.html.

21 Ibid.

22 Ibid.

23 Ibid.

24 Ibid.

25 Snyder, Bryan F. 'The Darwinian Nihilist Critique of Environmental Ethics.' *Ethics and the Environment* 22, no. 2 (Fall 2017): 59–78.

26 Laboria Cubonics. *The Xenofeminist Manifesto: A Politics for Alienation.* Verso, 2018, 1.

27 Žižek, Slavoj. *First as Tragedy, Then as Farce.* Verso, 2009, 97.

28 Desmond, William. *God and the Between.* John Wiley and Sons, 2008, 88.

29 Abbey, Edward. *Desert Solitaire.* University of Arizona Press, 1988, 6.

30 Ibid.

31 Roberts, Adam. *The Thing Itself.* Gollancz, 2016, 25.

32 Weil, Simone. *Gravity and Grace.* Routledge, 2002, 42.

33 Weil, Simone. *Waiting on God.* Collins, 1959, 43.

34 Ibid.

35 Von Hofmannsthal, Hugo. *The Lord Chandos Letter: And Other Writings.* NYRB Classics, 2007, 123.

36 Vila-Matas, Enrique. *Bartleby and Co.* Vintage, 2007, 89.

37 Agamben, George. *Remnants of Auschwitz: The Witness and the Archive.* Zone Books, 2000, 112.

38 Ibid., 117.

39 Vandermeer, Jeff. *Annihilation.* Fourth Estate, 2014.

40 Tompkins, David. 'Weird Ecology: On the Southern Reach Trilogy', *LARB*, 30 September 2014.

41 Rothman, Joshua. 'The Weird Thoreau', *The New Yorker*, 14 January 2015.

42 Tompkins, 'Weird Ecology'.

43 Morton, Timothy. *Hyperobjects: Philosophy and Ecology After the End of the World.* Stanford University Press, 2013, 81–95.

44 Tompkins, 'Weird Ecology'.

45 Ibid.

46 Foucault, Michel. *The Order of Things: An Archaeology of the Human Sciences.* Routledge, 2002, 422.

47 Nietzsche, Friedrich. *The Gay Science.* Cambridge University Press, 2001, 110.

48 www.lakedistrict.gov.uk/learning/geology

49 Weisman, Alan. *The World Without Us.* Thomas Dunne Books/St. Martin's Press, 2007.

50 Barnie, John. 'Just Words, That's All.' *Poetry Wales* 32, no. 4 (1997): 58.

51 Ibid.

52 Ibid.

53 Ibid.

54 Ibid., 59.

Sellafield

1 Wordsworth, William and Adam Sedgwick. *A Complete Guide to the Lakes...* *[with] Three Letters upon the Geology...by the Rev. Profssor Sedgwick.* Hudson & Nicholson, 1842, 15.

2 Wordsworth, William. *Poetical Works* eds. Thomas Hutchinson and Ernest de Sélincourt, vol. 2. Oxford University Press, 1936, 289–90.

3 Melville, Herman. *Moby-Dick or, the Whale.* Penguin, 2002, 525.

4 Miner, Earl. *The Japanese Tradition in British and American Literature.* Princeton University Press, 1958, 17.

5 Matsuo, Basho. *The Narrow Road to the Deep North, and Other Travel Sketches.* Penguin, 1966, 97.

6 Barthes, Roland. *Empire of Signs.* Hill and Wang, The Noonday Press, 1989, 30.

7 Ibid., 32.

8 Ibid., 3.

9 Ibid., 74–5.

10 Ibid., 83.

11 Nancy, Jean-Luc. *After Fukushima: The Equivalence of Catastrophe.* Fordham University Press, 2014, 9.

12 Ibid., 13.

13 Ibid., 14.

14 Matsuo, *Narrow Road*, 118.

15 Mahon, Derek. *The Snow Party.* Oxford University Press, 1975, 8.

16 De Angelis, Irene. *The Japanese Effect in Contemporary Irish Poetry.* Palgrave Macmillan, 2012, 51.

17 Ibid., 45.

18 Hilton, Tim. *John Ruskin.* Yale University Press, 2002, 864.

19 Williams, Jonathan. *Imaginary Postcards (Clints Grikes Grips Glints).* Trigram Press, 1975, 19.

20 McKie, Robin. 'Sellafield: The Most Hazardous Place in Europe', *The Guardian*, 19 April 2009.

21 Ibid.

22 Ibid.

23 Derrida, Jacques. 'No Apocalypse, Not Now (Full Speed Ahead, Seven Missiles, Seven Missives)'. *Diacritics* 14, no. 2 (1984): 20–31.

24 D'Agata, John. *About a Mountain.* W. W. Norton, 2011, 68.

25 Ibid., 178–9.

26 Searle, Adrian. 'Horribly Compelling: Bruce Conner's Nuclear Test Film Still Holds Us In Raptures', *The Guardian*, 15 June 2015.

27 Shurcliff, William. *Bombs at Bikini; the official report of Operation Crossroads, prepared under the direction of the Commander of Joint Task Force One, by W. A. Shurcliff, historian of Joint Task Force One.* H W Wise, 1947, 151–2.

28 Hales, Peter B. 'The Atomic Sublime.' *American Studies* 32, no. 1 (1991): 5.

29 Ibid., 12–3.

30 Sloterdijk, Peter. *Critique of Cynical Reason.* University of Minnesota Press, 1988, 130.

31 Tucci, Giuseppe. *The Religions of Tibet.* University of California Press, 1980, 63.

32 Derrida, Jacques. *Glas.* University of Nebraska Press, 1987, 238.

33 Thera, Nanamoli (trans.). *Three Cardinal Discourses of the Buddha.* Buddhist Publication Society, 1960, 7–8.

Bewcastle

1 Heidegger, Martin. *The Question Concerning Technology and Other Essays*, trans. William Lovitt. Harper, 1977, 8.

2 Hall, A. *Wreay.* Thurnam, 1929, 65.

3 Ibid., 66.

4 Uglow, Jenny. *The Pinecone: The Story of Sarah Losh, Romantic Heroine, Architect and Visionary.* Faber and Faber, 2013, 212.

5 Ibid., 212–3.

6 Ibid.

7 Ibid., 214.

8 Hall, *Wreay*, 56.

9 Burkett, Walter. *Ancient Mystery Cults.* Harvard University Press, 1989, 73.

10 https://romaninscriptionsofbritain.org/inscriptions/1546

11 Jeffers, Robinson. *The Selected Poetry of Robinson Jeffers.* Stanford University Press, 2002, 18.

12 July, Sharon. 'The Frontiers of the Roman Empire.' www.gounesco.com/the-frontiers-of-the-roman-empire/.

13 Pevsner, Nikolaus. *Cumberland and Westmorland: The Buildings of England.* Penguin, 1967, 15.

14 Collingwood, W.G. *The Ruskin Cross at Coniston Described and Illustrated.* W. Holmes, 1901, 4–5.

15 Bunting, Basil. *Briggflatts*. Bloodaxe Books, 2009, 13.

16 Burton, Richard. *A Strong Song Tows Us: The Life of Basil Bunting*. Infinite Ideas, 2013, 288–9.

17 Miller, J. Hillis. *Illustration*. Reaktion Books, 1992, 79.

18 Fellows, Jay. *Ruskin's Maze: Mastery and Madness in His Art*. Princeton University Press, 1981.

19 Derrida, Jacques. *Writing and Difference*. University of Chicago Press, 1978, 298.

20 Ruskin, John, Edward Tyas Cook, and Alexander D. O. Wedderburn. *The Works of John Ruskin*, Vol XXII. Library ed. George Allen; Longmans; Green, 1903, 45–2.

21 Ibid., 349–50.

22 Ibid., 322.

23 Miller, *Illustration*, 75.

24 Ruskin, *Works*, vol. XXII, 348.

25 Derrida, Jacques. *Of Grammatology*. University of Chicago Press, 1997, 287.

26 Morton, Timothy. *Dark Ecology: For a Logic of Future Coexistence*. Columbia University Press, 2016, 38ff.

27 Ibid., passim.

28 Ruskin, *Works*, vol. XXII, 319–20.

29 Ibid.

30 Ibid.

31 Heidegger, Martin. *Off the Beaten Track*. Cambridge University Press, 2002, 14.

32 Ruskin, *Works*, vol. XXII, 306.

33 Siegel, Jonah. 'Black Arts, Ruined Cathedrals, and the Grave in Engraving: Ruskin and the Fatal Excess of Art'. *Victorian Literature and Culture* 27, no. 2 (1999): 410.

34 Derrida, *Writing and Difference*, 303–4.

35 Johnson, Christopher. *System and Writing in the Philosophy of Jacques Derrida*. Cambridge University Press, 1993, 25.

36 Derrida, *Writing and Difference*, 304.

37 Orton, Fred, et al. *Fragments of History: Rethinking the Ruthwell and Bewcastle Monuments*. Manchester University Press, 2007, 30.

38 Ibid., 30.

39 Ibid., 31.

40 Bewcastlehouseofprayer.org.uk. 'The Vision'. www.bewcastlehouseofprayer.org.uk/the-vision/.

41 Ibid.

Boustead Hill

1 Clarke, David and Andy Roberts. 'The Solway Spaceman Photograph', *Fortean Times* 286, April 2012. https://drdavidclarke.co.uk/secret-files/the-solway-spaceman-photograph/.
2 Ibid.
3 Ibid.
4 Ibid.
5 Ibid.
6 www.uk-ufo.org/condign/casehoax.htm.
7 Ibid.
8 *Westmorland Gazette*, 'Coniston Old Man to Host Artist and UFO', 8 October 2004.
9 Bennett, Colin. *Looking for Orthon: The Story of George Adamski, the First Flying Saucer Contactee, and How He Changed the World.* Cosimo Books, 2008, 99–100.
10 Ibid., 207.
11 Richardson, Nick. 'Diary'. *London Review of Books* 40, no. 15, 2 August 2018.

Brantwood

1 Ruskin, John. *The Works of John Ruskin* eds. E. T. Cook and Alexander Wedderburn. George Allen, 1907, vol. XVII, 531.
2 Birch, Dinah. '"That Ghastly Work": Ruskin, Animals and Anatomy'. *Worldviews: Global Religions, Cultures, and Ecology* 4 (2000): 131–45.
3 Ruskin, John, Edward Tyas Cook, and Alexander D.O. Wedderburn, *The Works of John Ruskin*, Vol XXII. Library ed. George Allen; Longmans; Green, 1903, 237.
4 Birch, 'That Ghastly Work', 140.
5 Ibid., 142.
6 Potter, Beatrix. *The Journal of Beatrix Potter.* Frederick Warne, 1966, 70.
7 Deleuze, Gilles and Félix Guattari. *What Is Philosophy?* Verso, 1994, 109.
8 Agamben, George. *The Open: Man and Animal.* Stanford University Press, 2002.
9 Schaefer, Donovan. *Religious Affects: Animality, Evolution, and Power.* Duke University Press, 2015, 1–4.
10 Ibid., 128–9.

11 Ibid., 168.

12 Ibid., 129.

13 Agamben, Giorgio. Interview with Leyland de la Durantaye, *Bidou* no. 28. http://archive.bidoun.org/magazine/28-interviews/giorgio-agamben-with-leland-de-la-durantaye/.

Brigflatts

1 Fox, George. *Journal of George Fox*. Friends' Tract Assn., 1891, 109–10.

2 Ibid., 113–4.

3 Bunting, Basil. *Briggflatts*. Bloodaxe Books, 2009, 13.

4 Hinds, Hilary. *George Fox and Early Quaker Culture*. Manchester University Press, 2011, 72.

5 Agamben, George. *Potentialities: Collected Essays in Philosophy*. Stanford University Press, 1999, 45.

Dentdale

1 Fort, Charles. *The Book of the Damned*. Abacus, 1974, 115–6.

2 Ibid., 126.

3 Ibid.

4 Ibid., 127.

5 http://writingthemessianic.blogspot.com/2010/04/basil-bunting-and-jonathan-williams.html

6 Schlesinger, Kyle, 'The Jargon Society', *Jacket* 2, late 2009, http://jacketmagazine.com/38/jwd02-schlesinger.shtml.

7 Williams, Jonathan. *Imaginary Postcards (Clints Grikes Grips Glints)*. Trigram Press, 1975, 19.

8 Morgan, Robert. 'AN EAR IN BARTRAM'S TREE: Selected Poems, 1957–1967. By Jonathan Williams', *The Nation* 213, 1971, 189.

9 Williams, Jonathan. *ELITE/ELATE POEMS: Selected Poems 1971–75*. Jargon Society, 1979, 213.

10 Wyatt, John. *Reflections on the Lakes*. Cicerone Press, 1980, 163.

11 Ibid.

12 Ibid., 163–4.

13 Ibid., 165.

14 Blades, James. *Percussion Instruments and Their History*. Faber and Faber, 1984, 82.

15 Ruskin, John. *The Works of John Ruskin* eds. E. T. Cook and Alexander Wedderburn. George Allen, 1907, vol. XXVI, 115.

Coniston

1 Cormack, Sarah. *The Space of Death in Roman Asia Minor (Wiener Forschungen zur Archäologie, Bd. 6)*. Phoibos, 2009.
2 Leach, Neil, ed. *Rethinking Architecture: A Reader in Cultural Theory*. Routledge, 1997, 331.
3 Ibid.
4 Ibid., 332.
5 Ibid., 332–3.
6 Ibid., 333.
7 Hilton, Tim. *John Ruskin*. Yale University Press, 2002, 863.
8 Ibid., 494.
9 Leach, *Rethinking Architecture*, 336.
10 Freud, Sigmund. *The Complete Psychological Works of Sigmund Freud, Vol 18*. Vintage, 2001, 36.
11 Freud, Sigmund. *Civilisation and Its Discontents*. W. W. Norton & Co, 1985, 11.
12 Ibid., 21.
13 Theleweit, Klaus. *Male Fantasies Volume One: Women, Floods, Bodies, History*. University of Minnesota Press, 1987, 253.
14 Tremayne, David. *Donald Campbell: The Man Behind the Mask*. Bantam, 2004, 171.
15 Žižek, Slavoj. 'The Undergrowth of Enjoyment: How Popular Culture Can Serve as an Introduction to Lacan.' *New Formations* 9 (Winter 1989): 21.
16 Ibid., 21–2.
17 Loewenstein, Andrea Freud. *Loathsome Jews and Engulfing Women: Metaphors of Projection in the Works of Wyndham Lewis, Charles Williams, and Graham Greene*. New York University Press, 1995.
18 Theleweit, *Male Fantasies*, 283.

Elterwater

1 Wilson, Sarah. 'Kurt Schwitters in England.' *Tate Papers*, 2013.
2 Foster, Hal. *Postmodern Culture*. Pluto, 1985, 84.

3 Motherwell, Robert. *The Dada Painters and Poets: An Anthology*. Harvard University Press, 1989, 63.

4 Nancy, Jean-Luc and Aurelien Barrau. *What's These Worlds Coming To?* Fordham University Press, 2015, 48.

5 Ibid., 52.

6 Perloff, Marjorie. *The Futurist Movement: Avant-garde, Avant Guerre, and the Language of Rupture*. University of Chicago Press, 1986, 77.

7 Paulhan, Jean. *The Flowers of Tarbes, or, Terror in Literature*. University of Illinois Press, 2006, 31.

8 Wordsworth, William. *Poetical Works* eds. Thomas Hutchinson and Ernest de Sélincourt, vol. 2. Oxford University Press, 1952, 264.

Grange-over-Sands

1 Bucke, Richard. *Cosmic Consciousness: A Study in the Evolution of the Human Mind*. Causeway Books, 1974, xiii.

2 Carson, Rachel. *The Edge of the Sea*. Houghton Mifflin, 1955, vii.

3 Davis, David. 'Andrew Michael Hurley and "The Loney": An Interview with the Author of Tartarus' Newest Novel', *Weird Fiction Review*, 11 March 2015.

4 Heidegger, Martin. *On the Way to Language*. Harper and Row, 2003, 57.

5 Ashworth, Jenn. *Fell*. Sceptre, 2013.

6 Goldsmith, Kenneth. *Uncreative Writing*. Columbia University Press, 2011, 17.

7 Ibid., 18.

8 Fisher, Mark. *The Weird and the Eerie*. Repeater, 2016, 10–11.

9 Ibid., 13.

10 Ashworth, *Fell*, 38.

11 Ibid.

12 Ibid.

13 Ibid., 113.

14 Ibid.

15 Ibid., 114.

16 Ibid.

17 Ibid., 115.

18 Ibid., 172.

19 Ibid., 173.

20 Ibid.

21 Ibid., 174.

Ribblesdale

1 Derrida, Jacques. 'Force de Loi: Le Fondament Mystique De L'Autorité.' *Cardozo Law Review* 11 (1990): 1009.
2 Christopher, John. *The Death of Grass*. Penguin, 2009, 156.
3 Ibid., 172–3.
4 Ibid., 173.
5 Ibid., 191–2.
6 Wark, McKenzie. *Molecular Red: Theory for the Anthropocene*. Verso, 2015.
7 Coleman, Terry. *The Railway Navvies: A History of the Men Who Made the Railways*. Hutchinson, 1965, 192.
8 Ibid.
9 Ibid., 193.
10 Ibid.
11 Ibid., 194.

Sunderland Point

1 Gilroy, Paul. *The Black Atlantic: Modernity and Double Consciousness*. Harvard University Press, 1995.
2 Rice, Alan J. *Radical Narratives of the Black Atlantic*. Continuum, 2002, 213.
3 Patterson, Orlando. *Slavery and Social Death: A Comparative Study*. Harvard University Press, 1982, 13.
4 Ibid., 38.
5 Ibid.
6 Ibid., 39.
7 Ibid., 41.
8 Ibid., 46.
9 Ibid., 48.
10 Ibid.
11 Ibid., 50.
12 Ibid., 62.
13 Ibid., 61.
14 Ibid., 96.
15 Lyon, Kim. *Dentdale Bronte Trail*. Lyon Equipment, 1985.
16 Williams, Eric. *Capitalism & Slavery*. André Deutsch, 1964.
17 Wiener, Martin. *English Culture and the Decline of the Industrial Spirit, 1850–1980*. Penguin Books, 1985, 66.
18 Ibid.

Grizedale

1 Jung, Carl. *Memories, Dreams, Reflections*. Fontana, 1962, 223.
2 Ibid.
3 Ibid, 224.
4 Tufnell, Ben. Richard Long: Selected Statements & Interviews. Haunch of Venison, 2007, 39.
5 Grant, Bill and Paul Harris, eds. *The Grizedale Experience: Sculpture, Arts and Theatre in a Lakeland Forest*. Canongate, 1991, 8.
6 Ibid., 26.
7 Ibid., 38.
8 Ibid., 52.
9 Ibid., 86.
10 Artcornwall.org. 'Adam Sutherland on Grizedale, the Lake District and Rural Art'. www.artcornwall.org/interviews/Adam_Sutherland_Grizedale2.htm.
11 Haslam, Dave. *Not Abba*. Fourth Estate, 2005.
12 Ford, Simon. *Wreckers of Civilisation: The Story of COUM Transmissions & Throbbing Gristle*. Black Dog Publishing, 1999, 6.22.
13 Walker, John. *Left Shift: Radical Arts in 1970s Britain*. Tauris, 2001.

Water Yeat

1 Griffin, Jonathan and Adam Sutherland. *Grizedale Arts: Adding Complexity to Confusion*. Grizedale Arts, 2009, 178–9.
2 Ibid., 179.
3 Ibid., 180.
4 Ibid., 180.
5 Ibid, 179–80.
6 Hall, Sarah. *The Carhullan Army*. Faber and Faber, 2007; Haushofer, Marlen. *The Wall*. Quartet, 2013.

Happy Mount Park

1 Kolbert, Elizabeth. 'Britain's Answer to Barney', *New York Times*, 27 March 1994.
2 www.thevisitor.co.uk/news/morecambe-and-the-blobby-land-saga-20-years-on-1-6755475

3 Bataille, Georges. *Visions of Excess: Selected Writings, 1927–1939.* University of Minnesota Press, 1985, 31.

4 Lispector, Clarice. *The Passion According to G.H.* New Directions, 2012, 171.

5 Ibid., 188.

6 Preil, Joseph J. ed. *Holocaust Testimonies: European Survivors and American Liberators in New Jersey.* Rutgers University Press, 2001, 46.

7 Adorno, Theodor W. *Prisms.* MIT Press, 1981, 34.

8 Hartman, Geoffrey. Holocaust Remembrance: The Shapes of Memory. 1994, 22.

9 Snyder, Timothy. *Black Earth: The Holocaust as History and Warning.* Vintage, 2016, 4.

10 Blanchot, Maurice. *The Writing of the Disaster.* University of Nebraska Press, 1986, 47.

11 Rukeyser, Muriel. *Out of Silence.* Northwestern University Press, 151.

12 Lispector, *Passion*, 67.

13 Moser, Benjamin. *Why This World: A Biography of Clarice Lispector.* Oxford University Press, 2009, 266.

14 Lispector, *Passion*, 40.

15 Ungar-Sargon, Batya. 'The Man Who Loves Women', *Tablet Magazine*, 17 August 2014. www.tabletmag.com/jewish-arts-and-culture/books/ 181490/moser-sontag.

16 Braidotti, Rosi. *Metamorphoses: Towards a Materialist Theory of Becoming.* Polity, 2002.

17 Ibid., 48.

18 Shaviro, Steven. 'Two Lessons from Burroughs' in Halberstam, Judith and Ira Livingston (eds.), *Posthuman Bodies.* Indiana University Press, 1995, 47.

19 Ibid., 48.

20 Ibid., 53.

21 Ibid., 53–4.

22 Ibid., 54.

Conclusion

1 Dyer, Geoff. *Zona: A Book about a Film about a Journey to a Room.* Canongate, 2013, 47–8.

2 Ibid., 58.

3 Ibid., 63.

Unidentified Fictional Objects appear in the spaces in between established genres and disciplines including fact and fiction, theory and practice, past and future, science and sociology, art and academia.

We believe that stories can be both provocative and engaging, especially when they use new methodologies and modes of communication to challenge current distributions of power and knowledge.

We seek objects that may (or may not) resemble science fiction, critical utopias, creative dystopias, speculative writing, weird fiction, weird non-fiction.

We publish things (print, digital, plus) of varying lengths and call out to writers and readers who no longer wish to be constrained by categories.

UFOs speculate, reinvent, weird and undo economies, societies, environments, identities and sexualities. They appeal to students and their teachers, friends, and relations (human and otherwise).